BRUCHE

A Collection of Memories
1942 - 2006

By
Mary G. Randles

First Published 2006 by Countyvise Limited,
14 Appin Road, Birkenhead, Wirral CH41 9HH.

Copyright © 2006 Mary Randles

The right of Mary Randles
to be identified as the author of this work has been asserted by her in accordance with the Copyright, Design and
Patents Act 1988.

British Library Cataloguing in Publication Data.
A catalogue record for this book is available from the British Library.

Please note: From 1st January 2007 ISBNs will contain 13 numbers these numbers will be the same as the present
number printed below the barcode (ie. starting 978).
Countyvise is showing both existing (10 digit) and future (13 digit) ISBNs on the Title page verso. Please continue
to use the 10 figure number until 31st December 2006.

ISBN 1 901231   ISBN 978 1 901231

Acknowledgements

When I first had the idea to compile a history of Bruche, I never imagined that it would develop so quickly and so far.

From my first tentative enquiries among friends and colleagues who had passed through there, as students or trainers, I have been very fortunate to speak to some wonderful people all over the world about their times at the centre, and enjoyed some great conversations with them.

I am very much indebted to all those people who have allowed me to use their treasured photographs of moments at Bruche in this book, and also to those who have taken the time and trouble to record and pass on their memories of their times there so that I could achieve my goal of compiling this history and memories of Bruche.

Particular thanks are due to the following, whose help (and patience!) have enabled me to complete this project:

- The staff at Bruche Police Training Centre who have allowed me to ferret through their dusty archives in search of information

- Bert Gaskin and Cyril Mills, who were a mine of information about the first days of police training at Bruche

- Alan Spiers who took so many photographs for me

- Aldon P. Ferguson who has been a constant source of information and assistance about RAF Burtonwood, Bruche Hall and the US staff who lived and worked there

- The Burtonwood Heritage Museum, whose staff were of such great assistance at the start of my research

- The Burtonwood Association who have assisted with contacts and help to trace Bruche Hall residents from prior to 1946

- NARPO Magazine whose publication of my appeal for information resulted in contacts with retired officers from all over the world

- The Caminada Society whose members gave me so much information about their experiences at Bruche

- Warren J. Kellerman, who provided me with information about life at Bruche Hall from 1942 to 1946, and a copy of his book 'Station X' which was a mine of information on US personnel at Bruche Hall

- All the former staff and students of Bruche, without whose memories and assistance this book would not have been possible

- Jim W. Lee who provided information and photographs from Station X

- Sgt. Tracy L. English, Clarence Hightower and Gene Wallace who assisted in providing me with photographs from Kelly AFB

- The GMP Museum who helped me with information about former Manchester officers

Dedication

This book is dedicated to the many thousands of police officers who have passed through Bruche Police Training Centre, and who have faithfully carried out the duty of constable according to its original definition:

A constable is a citizen, locally appointed, but having authority under the Crown

for the protection of life and property;

the maintenance of order;

the prevention and detection of crime;

and the prosecution of offenders against the peace

Foreword - Chief Inspector Phil Jones, Head of Centre 2006

There have been 17 Commandants or Heads of Centre at the Police Training Centre at Bruche of which I am the last.

My distinguished predecessors established and oversaw a dynamic and vibrant training environment which served the North West Police region for over 60 years. It has been my privilege to take on their mantle, although sadly, only to oversee the Centre to a position of closure.

There is a long and dignified history at Bruche, beginning in the war years with American Air Force personnel and shortly afterwards continuing with police training.

The first probationer constables arrived in January 1946 and it is no exaggeration to state the majority of police officers, perhaps tens of thousands serving in the North West police forces, were trained at Bruche.

In the same period hundreds of staff, both police and civilian, entered our gates and found a working environment where friendships flourished, where births, deaths, marriage and divorce were shared amongst caring colleagues.

Hard work and enthusiasm for the business of the Centre has always been endemic amongst Bruche people. Such a family atmosphere fostered many events and encounters.

I am delighted that someone has taken the time and made the effort to collate all those anecdotes and memories into an order which forms an easy read, creating visions in the mind of the reader that will bring a smile to many.

I commend this work to all who have connections with Bruche.

Phil Jones - Head of Centre. May 2006

The main roundabout at Bruche, 2006

Bruche

Bruche is the name of an ancient manor within the parish of Warrington, as well as the name of a family who belonged to that manor for more than 300 years, until the reign of Queen Elizabeth I.

Bruche Hall was the seat of the Bruche family until the manor was sold to Peter Legh of Bradley, early in the 17th century.

By the beginning of the 19th century, the estate and hall were owned by a soap manufacturer, Jonathon Jackson. Jackson became bankrupt, as a result of action by excise officers, and in 1824 the Bruche estate was bought by Thomas Parr for the sum of £19,200.

In 1908 the hall was occupied by a Colonel J. D. Buckton, and subsequently became a convent. The hall, together with 11 acres of grounds had been bought by the Roman Catholic Church for educational purposes. The lands included the site for the building of St. Oswald's Church, the foundation stone for which was laid on May 29th 1927 by the then Archbishop of Liverpool, Dr. Keating.

Near to the site of Bruche Hall, a collection of buildings was erected in 1940/41 to provide accommodation for workers employed in wartime production of munitions at Risley, but they were never used for this purpose.

In 1942, the Americans came to Burtonwood air base, which was the biggest air base in the world, outside of the States. Accommodation at Burtonwood was at a premium, and American personnel were based at several camps around the Warrington area. The sites were purely living sites with no work of any description going on there.

The collection of buildings at what was to become the No. 1 District Police Training Centre, Bruche was acquired by the US Army Authorities as an accommodation camp, and was called Bruche Hall. Bruche Hall, Canada Hall and several others all shared the same design in the theatres which were erected on the sites.

Canada Hall was occupied by the British, and or Canadian, Army before 1942 and was made available to the US when they joined the war and arrived at Burtonwood. Mostly it was used by women (Women's Army Corps) who were transported to and from Burtonwood daily. Bruche Hall was used by men.

The Halls, including Bruche, were a complete living site with living accommodation, messes etc. Some of the original buildings, including the theatre still exist at Bruche, and were in daily use until the centre closed in 2006.

From the entrance to Bruche Hall, looking towards the theatre – circa 1942

BRUCHE HALL ORGANISATIONAL CHART 1942

Captain Franklin Weir
Commanding Officer
Provost Marshal
PX Officer

Mr. Lester J. Milhan
Executive Officer

Mr. Lester R. Landrum
Adjutant Officer

Mr. H. G. Coffman
Asst. Adjutant Officer
Officer in Charge of Personnel
Censor Officer

Mr. Walter Gunkel
Asst. Adjutant
(Camp Administration)

Lt. Freigel
Mess Officer

Mr. J. R. James
Officer in Charge of Barracks

Mr. A. B. Norris
Officer in Charge of Barracks Inspection

Mr. Steve White
Fire Marshal

Mr. Fritz Reuter
Chemical Warfare Officer

Mr. H. A. Schramm
Transportation Officer, Supply

Mr. W. C. Stores
Transportation Officer, Engineering

History of Station X

In July 1942, the San Antonio Air Depot (SAAD) in Duncan Field, Texas was ordered to recruit, assemble and dispatch a group of 1050 trained and experienced civilian technician volunteers to a foreign service duty station. Their mission was to ensure that all aircraft and related combat equipment were combat ready at all times.

This duty station was given the code designation of 'Station X'. Volunteers had no idea of where they were going, or what to expect when they got there, until the ocean going vessels docked in Liverpool, England, or in Gourock, Scotland.

Some of the volunteers were transported in a ship called the Reina del Pacifico, others were transported on the Queen Elizabeth.

The Reina Del Pacifico was built in 1931 by Harland and Wolff in Belfast for the Pacific Steam Navigation Company (P.S.N.C.). She was PSNC's largest vessel at the time, the first with a white hull. She was also the first PSNC passenger ship name that didn't begin with 'O'. Her maiden voyage was from Liverpool to Valparaiso.

In December 1939 she was converted into a troopship at Liverpool. On 6th August 1942, she left Liverpool for North America to fetch U.S. and Canadian troops to Britain. The exact date of her arrival back in Liverpool, loaded with troops and civilian technicians, is thought to have been on or around the 5th September 1942.

Warren J. Kellerman was one of the people in the first group of civilian technician volunteers who were transported on the Reina Del Pacifico, and he describes his experiences of being recruited and transported to Station X in his book:

'Upon obtaining a balanced team of specialists numbering approximately 1050 volunteers, we were processed through the medical department for exams, inoculations and vaccinations. We then received lists of suggested clothing and baggage to take, and told when we might expect to depart.

On the morning of August 13, 1942 our first group of Station X volunteers (500) boarded a Southern Pacific train parked on the tracks inside Duncan Field.

The train trip to New York took approximately three days. Personnel were assigned lodgings at the Lincoln Hotel, where we stayed for two days. We boarded a Spanish ship named Reina del Pacifico (Queen of the Pacific) during the night of the second day. Awakening the next morning we found ourselves at sea.

Upon reaching Halifax, Nova Scotia, we joined a larger convoy with an escort of US Navy war ships. German submarines were a constant menace during our voyage. We viewed depth charges exploding in the distance almost daily. Some of those in our group witnessed the sinking of a German sub. One night around midnight a torpedo also hit one of the ships to the port side of the Reina del Pacifico.

After 13 days at sea we entered the Crosbey (sic) Channel on the River Mersey. Bombed and sunken ships littered the harbour. Such devastation, along with the various German sub encounters while crossing the Atlantic, brought the harsh realities of war into full focus.

The ship docked at night and we learned from the people on the wharf that we were in Liverpool, England. After disembarking we marched to double decker buses waiting to take us to Cadishead. After two days the group was moved to permanent quarters at Bruche Hall in Warrington, England, approximately four miles from our work site at BRD.'

At this time the site at Bruche Hall consisted of six double wings and one single wing, single storey barracks, identified alphabetically from A to M. These barracks incorporated steam heated, dormitory type bedrooms (two to three men to a room) with a central bath room in each wing.

2nd Lt. Jack Hill looking west from the theatre roof (1942).

In the previous photograph, the barracks accommodation can be clearly seen, together with some of the housing that still surrounds the site.

The administrative building consisted of a large, one storey brick building which contained the kitchen, mess hall, US Army Post Office, Post Exchange, auditorium (used for church services and entertainment), personnel office and clinic. The clinic was staffed by Army medical personnel.

Towards the theatre from the Officers Quarters (July 1942)

The previous photograph shows the theatre (auditorium), the administrative building is out of picture on the right, behind the barracks which can just be seen to the far right of the picture.

The second group of 312 technicians, under the leadership of Fred Wendt left SAAD on 25th August 1942, a third group of 124 radio technicians from Texas, New York and Pennsylvania followed on 28th October 1942.

The fourth and final group of 114 aircraft instrument technicians under the leadership of Howard Schramm and assistant Walter Gunkel left on 26th December 1942.

Howard Schramm describes his arrival at Bruche Hall as follows;

'The group arrived in Scotland during the night. Everyone was told to carry his own duffel bag and a box of 'C' rations for the transfer from the ship to the passenger train that took us south to Warrington, England. It was raining when we arrived and were trucked to Bruche Hall. Reaching our destination around midnight, we assembled in the Mess Hall for spam sandwiches and were then assigned to M Barracks.'

The civilian technicians from Bruche Hall, and personnel from other Halls in the area, were bussed into Burtonwood Base daily to work, and then returned to their camp at the end of their shift.
They wore military uniforms, although they were not service personnel, the US Headquarters in London having ordered that all civil service technicians be directed to buy and wear US Army uniforms during their assignment in Britain.

This direction probably arose following Hitler's order that, in the event of an invasion of Britain, the Home Guard Rank or Class (British) would be shot, and it was thought likely that this edict would include all the SAAD civilian technicians wearing civilian clothes.

Guard Inspection by Lt. Col. Wogan and Lt. Col. McManus (Aug.1942)

The roundabout at Bruche Hall outside the theatre (1942)

The administrative building is to the right of the theatre, behind the car and jeep.

Lysle R. Turnbeaugh was a sergeant in the US Army Air Corps stationed at Bruche Hall from early 1944 until the US personnel left in October 1945.

During the time he was there he was assigned the duty of securing food and turning it over to the mess sergeant for preparation for the troops that were then being processed through the site – the site was known as a reinforcement depot.

The reinforcement depot received new troops from the US to be processed and sent on to their permanent assignments, housing, feeding and clothing them for their respective units.

As the war was drawing to an end, the site was re-classified as a replacement depot, and received and processed troops that were being sent back to the States.

Lysle describes the accommodation as being in nissen huts, where they were assigned two people to a room. There was a bunk bed (upper and lower) and the rooms were pretty small. However the bathroom facilities were good, with large bath tubs and plenty of hot water.

As Lysle was responsible for the ordering and transporting of food into the camp, he says he can account for its quality. There was plenty of ground meat, eggs, bread from a large bakery in Aintree and lots of potatoes, Brussels sprouts etc. He doesn't recall many complaints from the troops about the food, so it must have been OK!

While stationed at Bruche Hall, Lysle met his wife, Gladys Rose who lived on Princess Avenue, Warrington, and they were married in Warrington on 1st December 1945. They now live in California, and celebrate 60 years of marriage on 1st December 2005.

Lysle's was the first of many stories of romance and marriage begun at Bruche that I discovered during my research.

I also discovered that the author of 'Station X', Warren Kellerman, also met and married his wife Marjorie during his time at Bruche Hall. Marjorie was a secretary at Burtonwood, and was originally from Rainhilll, Merseyside, where the couple married.

Mr. and Mrs. Kellerman have very kindly allowed me to include their wedding photograph in my book, and I am pleased to include it as a reminder of the very many happy times and occasions that have been a part of Bruche's history over the years.

No doubt there are many, many more stories of love and marriage during the 60+ years Bruche has been accommodating service personnel and police officers. Was it something in the air, or the water………………..?

Entertainment

Dancing in the theatre (Exact date unknown, thought to be 1942 – 1944)

The bands from the base at Burtonwood would play in the theatre regularly and men and women from the local RAF and RN bases at Padgate and Stretton etc. would be invited and vice versa.

One of the bands who played at the theatre at Bruche Hall was Eddie Kistler's Swing Tips, who had also played at RAF Burtonwood and locally in Warrington.

Frank Otero, the saxophonist with the Swing Tips, who now lives in a nursing home in New York, landed in Gourock, Scotland on 1st November 1943, as he said 'after 10 days of crossing the Atlantic dodging German subs'. Frank recalls that the band used to play for dances at Parr Hall, and that they were very popular in many towns locally, especially at the Red Cross Club in Manchester, which he recalls being near St. Anne Street and Cross Street in Manchester. The band also played at the Palladium with Vera Lynn and Ann Shelton.

Certain American entertainers also visited Canada and Bruche Halls, one of whom was Broderick Crawford, a famous TV personality of the time, who played Chief Dan Mathews in the TV series Highway Patrol in the1960s.

Some of the personnel from Bruche Hall would probably have been in the audience at Burtonwood for one of Glenn Miller's band's last concerts. Miller's band had played at Warton (now BAE systems), near Preston, Lancashire, and then flown to Burtonwood for another concert.

From Burtonwood the band then flew to Bedford, from where on December 15th 1944 Miller set off on his final flight – never to be seen again.

'Flying Rumours'

This was the newspaper of Station X, a weekly publication circulated to the residents of Bruche Hall. It carried news, weather reports, cartoons and jokes, together with rumours that would circulate about events that may have happened.

The issue dated 19th April 1943, carries the following notices, which appear to show that Bruche Hall may have been in the grip of a mini crime wave:

'$5.00 REWARD

Five dollars reward for information leading to the recovery of a bicycle which was taken from G Barracks Sunday, April 4th between 6:00pm and 10:00pm. Anyone having any information please submit it to Joseph Smith, G – 30'.

'RETURN SPECIAL SERVICE EQUIPMENT

Joe Necker, Special Service Head, requests that the playing shoes, approximately 20 pairs, and the balls and other equipment which were borrowed from the Special Service Office be returned immediately. Fellows, this equipment belongs to everybody, and the stock must be kept on hand in order that everyone may benefit from its presence, not just a few'.

On September 20th 1943, the following announcement was the first item on the newspaper; it would appear that the barracks were not being kept as clean and tidy as they should have been:

'SANITATION

Your room, your barracks, this entire camp is considered your home and should be treated as such. Cleanliness is considered next to godliness and if that is true there are a few individuals in this camp who are going to hell.

Open your blackout curtains, keep at least the small window open at all times, make your beds, sweep the floor, keep the room tidy and clothes neatly arranged.

A formal inspection of this site will be made every Saturday commencing at 1000 hours. This will include inspection of all barracks and rooms. In addition there will be daily checks of the barracks and rooms. Your health is at stake and every precaution should be taken by you to insure and safeguard yourself".

The resulting inspection caught several out, as the results which follow show:

'SATURDAY INSPECTION RESULTS

BARRACKS	*REMARKS*
A	*Very Good*
B	*Good*
C	*Poor*
D	*Good*
E	*Excellent*
F	*Very Good*
G	*Very Good*
H	*Good*
I	*Good*
J	*Very Good*
K	*Good*
L	*Very Good*
M	*Very Good'*

Another worry for the personnel, apart from the cleanliness of their accommodation was personal hygiene, sex and morality. An event announced in the 19th April 1943 edition of Flying Rumours illustrates this:

'SAD SACK SHOW'

There will be a Hygeine and Sex Morality show presented this week. This show will be given by Chaplain Oakley Lee, and every member of this contingent is advised that it will be imperative for them to attend this lecture.

Anyone not attending will render himself subject to a seven day confinement to camp, as these shows are given purely to benefit each individual in this organisation, both physically and morally, by presenting them with exact information in connection with present conditions. Announcements will be made as to the exact date'.

The sense of humour of personnel at Bruche Hall resulted in several jokes and cartoons being published in the Flying Rumours, and I have chosen my personal favourite to include here:

SIDELIGHT

This sign is reported displayed in our Barber Shop: "In case of an air raid, crawl under the slot machine; the jackpot hasn't been hit in five years."

The men of Station X provided urgently needed mission support services during a crucial phase of the war in Europe, prior to the arrival of military technicians.

Their actions made a difference and helped to turn the tide for the allied forces.

The following quotation is from a letter of appreciation, sent to the family of each civil service technician during his tour of duty at Station X:

'I wish to thank you, who are closest to him, for the sacrifices you are making due to his overseas duty with this organization, and to assure you he is performing his duties well. His patriotism, loyalty and devotion to our country, the United States of America, deserves recognition, and he, being in the position of the man, behind the man, behind the gun, may be overlooked by some. He will get no medals and will not be acclaimed a hero by the newspapers; only in the eyes of you and a few of us who know the entire circumstances relative to this group, and the difficulties and complex situations encountered on their missions, will his services be fully appreciated.'

Lester J. Milhan, Superintendent
July 14, 1942

A commemorative brick in memory of all those who served at Station X, is located at the Veterans Monument Plaza at Kelly Air Force Base in San Antonio, Texas.

In the colour photographs section of this book, there are 2 photographs showing the Veterans Memorial at Kelly Air Force Base in San Antonio, and the memorial brick. These were very kindly taken for me by Sgt. Tracy L. English from Lackland Air Force Base in Texas, and by Gene Wallace, a retired police officer from San Antonio, Texas.

US personnel finally left Bruche Hall in October 1945, and the site was handed back to the War Department.

1946 – 1949

On 28th January 1946, the site, then comprising some 16 acres, was opened as a police training centre and the first police recruits began their training there.

The centre initially had responsibility for training recruits at both initial and continuation levels for the forces in the counties of Cheshire, Cumberland, Lancashire, Westmorland and the Isle of Man, although recruits from many of the forces in England and Wales were also trained there over the years.

The first Commandant in charge of the centre was Percy Hawkins, a former Chief Constable of the Glossop force.

Mr. Hawkins was the longest serving Commandant at Bruche, having been in the post from 1946 to 1954, approximately 8 years.

Percy Hawkins – First Commandant of the Police Training Centre, Bruche

The picture above shows Constable Albert (Bert) Gaskin from the Manchester City Police (left of photo) and a colleague who are booking in with Inspector Hunt at the centre reception desk as they arrive to begin their training on 28th January 1946.

Bert had joined the Manchester City force, and arrived at their headquarters in South Street, Manchester on the morning of the 28th January 1946, from where all the new recruits were bussed to Bruche to begin their training.

There were 4 classes on the first intake of recruits at Bruche, A, B, C and D. Bert was assigned to B Class, with Inspector Hunt as his instructor. Another officer on that first intake was Cyril Mills, a recruit from Liverpool City police. He was assigned to A Class.

Cyril and Bert are on the photograph of the first recruits and staff at Bruche, which is shown on the following page, and also on their respective class photographs.

Both Bert and Cyril have been an excellent source of information and help with this book, and I am very much indebted to them for that. Both were guests at the Golden Jubilee Parade at Bruche in 1996, and at the final pass out parade on 26th May 2006, so maintaining the links between past and present at the centre.

First recruits and staff at Bruche – January 1946.
Constable Cyril Mills (Liverpool City) - 6th from the right on the third row from the front

'A' Class – Course 1
Cyril Mills (Liverpool City) is 4th from the left on the back row.

'B' Class – Course 1. Bert Gaskin is on the far left of the back row

'D' Class – Course 1

Below are the requirements for a constable with the Manchester City Police in 1946 which Bert had to fulfil before being accepted.

MANCHESTER CITY POLICE

INFORMATION FOR THE GUIDANCE OF APPLICANTS

A candidate for appointment must be of good character and possess the following qualifications:

a)   British Nationality
b)   Age – between 20 and 30 years
c)   Good health (A medical examination will be carried out by the Police Surgeon before appointment)
d)   Good physique – deflated chest measurement not below 36 inches
e)   Height – not less than 5 feet 10 inches
f)   A good standard of education (A candidate will be required to pass an examination in educational subjects).

No candidate will be accepted without making personal application at Police Headquarters, South Street, Manchester. Expenses incurred in attending will not be paid by Police.

A candidate is required to produce three references covering about ten years. Where an applicant has served in H.M. Forces, the Certificate of Discharge is to be produced.

Information regarding pay and allowances and general Conditions of Service will be given to the candidate before final acceptance.

Bert remembers that, contrary to what the final paragraph of the information says, he had no idea of what his pay would be until he was actually at Bruche, in the classroom with the other members of his class. It was then that he found out he would be paid £4 2s 6d per week.

Frank Wright of the Lancashire Constabulary, who was at Bruche in June 1948 recalls that the requirements for Lancashire recruits of the time also included that they weren't allowed to have false teeth or wear glasses.

Recruits from Course 1 in the assembly hall for the Commandant's welcome speech, January 28th 1946

Another view of the recruits listening to the Commandant's speech
Cyril Mills is 4th from left on front row

An official opening of the training centre took place on Monday 4th February 1946, with 130 recruits on parade on the cindered parade ground. The weather at the time was described as gusty and bitterly cold.

The recruits had served in various branches of the forces during the war, and some proudly displayed their military decorations on their new police uniforms.

The centre was officially opened by Major M. J. Egan, HM Inspector of Constabulary. Others present included more than 30 police chiefs from county, city and borough forces in the area, and Mr. M. G. Russell, a representative from the Home Office.

The Centre Commandant, Mr. Percy Hawkins was also present, together with his deputy, Superintendent C. V. Hegg from Liverpool.

In his speech to the new recruits, Major Egan said,

"Remember first of all that you are public servants. You will be taught the law, which gives you great power over your fellow citizen. But you have to use that power with the utmost discretion. The people of this country are naturally the most law-abiding in the world. They require little chivvying to get them to obey the law. By your courtesy and consideration, you can get them in the right way to observe the law. In some countries the police dominate the people. That is one thing in this country we must always avoid. People will react if you approach them in the right manner".

Captain A. F. Hordern, chief constable of Lancashire, referring to a crime wave taking place at the time, is reported to have said that such things were always to be expected as an aftermath of war.

He said it was difficult to assess which was the most important to police officers duties – the prevention of crime or the prevention of death and injury on the roads. Given the manpower and the tools, the police could play a vital role in the prevention of those ghastly tragedies taking place on the roads of this country day after day.

Mr. T. C. Griffiths, chief constable of Chester, and an officer of some 40 years experience advised the recruits to do their best to their fellow men.

Although there were many police officers at Bruche, it is important not to forget the other members of staff, without whom the centre could not have functioned.

The photograph below shows some of the instructors from the centre at the time, with Annie Ballatti, who was one of the housekeeping staff. It is believed to be from early 1946.

Annie Ballatti and members of Instructional Staff – circa 1946
Reproduced by kind permission of Audrey Ballatti

Mrs. Ballatti was one of several members of the housekeeping staff to receive the Imperial Service Medal. The Imperial Service Order was created in 1902 with one level of award – Companion – and a medal for civil servants.

The Companion award ceased to be used in the United Kingdom in 1993, but the Imperial Service Medal continues to be awarded to civil servants who have completed 25 years of service in a non-managerial grade.

One of Mrs. Ballatti's duties at Bruche was to take the Inspectors' white collars to the Chinese Laundry in Padgate, where they would be washed and starched. She would then have to return and collect them, and take them back for the Inspectors to wear with their uniforms.

This must have been quite a lucrative contract for the Chinese Laundry, as there were at least 25 Inspectors employed at Bruche, not to mention the Commandant and his Deputy!

Annie Ballatti is presented with her Imperial Service Medal.

Housekeeping staff at Bruche in the 1950s – the centre matron, Miss Wright is seated to the Commandant' (Mr. Seward)'s right. On his left is the Deputy Commandant, Mr. O'Keefe.

Life at Bruche in the 1940s

The photograph below is of 'O' Class, Course 13, who were at the centre from 29th July 1946 until 26th October 1946. My-father-in-law, PC 141 Thomas Randles, is pictured second from the left on the back row. He was an officer from the Salford City Police, who had 7 officers on Course 13.

Other officers in this intake of recruits came from Barrow (9), Oldham (5), St. Helens (2) and Stockport (1) Borough Police Forces. The instructor was Herbert J. Sutton, from Manchester City Police, who is pictured in the centre of the front row.

O Class, Course 10.

Sixth from the right on the back row is Constable George Briggs from Salford City Police, who has assisted me by providing some of his memories of his time at Bruche.

Police training in 1946 began with a 14 week training course at training centres like Bruche. At this time, the centre had classrooms, dining halls, residential and sleeping quarters with modern amenities, and recreational facilities. It had bedroom accommodation for 262 students and 22 members of staff.

Each recruit had their own bedroom, within a large, chalet type building, with central heating. The centre of the building was a passage way, on the wall of which was a notice board. Each man would have to be back on the centre by 10.30 pm and sign in on the notice board. Officers who failed to do this would be subjected to disciplinary procedures.

Washrooms in the accommodation buildings were partitioned into cubicles, with mirrors. The classrooms were furnished with individual desks and chairs, and it was reported that those chairs had cushions!

There were 2 dining halls, where meals for 420 people could be served, and there were always second helpings for those with larger appetites. The food has been described as similar to what the recruits had been used to in the Armed Forces, and there was still severe rationing in place. One dining hall was a 'wet' canteen, where there was a bar which opened around 6pm.
Recruits were expected to be in the dining hall a few minutes before meal times to await the arrival of the Commandant, and they were unable to leave before he did.

A description of the facilities at the time reported that there were postal and library facilities, billiards room, a theatre and cinema hall for concerts and dances, which was completely equipped with full stage effects, artistes rooms and projection room. A separate hut was available for games, and there was a hairdressing saloon and showers.

Recruits playing snooker in the snooker hall

Recruits reading in the reception area 1946

Teaching the recruits was carried out by twenty five inspectors and sergeants, seconded from their respective forces, and they instructed the recruits in first aid, physical training, drill, swimming, police procedure and administration, civic duties and road safety.

Recruits were instructed in lifesaving and swimming skills at Warrington swimming baths, and would be taken there by bus from the centre. It was expected that all police constables would be able to swim, and it is thought that some of those who still could not swim on their return to force from Bruche would have been sacked.

Percy Grierson of the Lancashire Constabulary was fortunate enough to be able to swim, and he, along with many others, left Bruche in late 1947 with an Elementary Certificate from the Royal Lifesaving Society which was awarded for *'Passing the elementary tests of the society in lifesaving, surface diving, swimming, and the resuscitation of the apparently drowned'.*

Specialists were invited to give lectures on other relevant subjects, and PC Briggs recalls that he and his fellow recruits were instructed on the Diseases of Animals Act, including the laws relating to sheep dipping. However, he and his colleagues from Salford City Police were not tested on their knowledge of this legislation, as there were no sheep in Salford!

Bert Gaskin recalls how the Commandant, Mr. Hawkins, was famous for his lectures on foot and mouth disease, which he delivered personally to each class. General opinion among the recruits from the city forces was that a foot and mouth epidemic had been the biggest thing to happen in the Commandant's career with the Glossop force (it being somewhat rural in the area it covered) and that he was making the most of telling the recruits about it. Word would be passed around the centre – 'He's done us, you're next, don't fall asleep!'

Another regular specialist visitor who gave lectures to the recruits was Dr. Firth from the forensic science laboratory. He would lecture on forensic investigation, and show graphic colour slides to illustrate his lectures. On one occasion a male recruit fainted during the slide show, and was summoned to see the Commandant. As a result of having fainted at the slides, his career as a police constable was terminated, as he could be expected to see sights like this and worse during police work. Police constables were expected to be able to deal with such situations without fainting.

Recruits also visited assize and magistrates courts during their training, to see how justice was done there.

Classes began at 9am and ended at 5.15pm, and there was much to learn. A poster of the time showed 13 different types of bicycle handlebars, all named, and which all had to be memorised. No doubt such information would have greatly assisted the officers during the role play shown in the following photograph.

Rough notes would be made in class, and the evening would be spent writing them out in longhand into a hardback exercise book, provided for the purpose. Recruits spent all day in class, except for Wednesday afternoons, when they had to go outside, either to play sport or go for a walk.

In October 1947, Birrell Shorrock, a recruit from the Lancashire Constabulary, remembers playing football on Wednesday afternoons, but that they had no football kit, and had to play in their shirt sleeves or vests, county flannels (uniform trousers) and police boots. He also recalls that no-one suffered serious injury as a result of this and that all the recruits went on to pass out at the end of their training.

There were occasional moments of light relief, one of which was described by Roly Mason of the Manchester City force, who began his training at Bruche on March 11th 1946.

Roly recalled that they were outside one of the accommodation blocks, having some practical instruction on gaining entry to premises from one of the instructors, who was usually described as being rather pompous.

A recruit was instructed to knock on the door of the block, as if trying to gain entry, which he duly did.

The instructor thought his attempt to be rather too timid and quiet, and bustled forward, announcing, "Not like that, I'll show you how it should be done!" He then knocked loudly on the door of the block.

Seconds later, as he was about to explain how to gain entry, the door burst open and two female members of the cleaning staff appeared in the doorway, armed with brushes. They then proceeded to beat the instructor with the brushes, very much as Nora Batty would have done to Compo in the TV show *Last of the Summer Wine!*

Much laughter ensued, and a good point was made too, about the type of things that could happen when officers attempted to gain entry to premises.

Further light relief came from giving nicknames to instructors. It is rumoured that the first aid instructor during this first decade of police training at Bruche was referred to as 'Crepitus' or 'Excroooooooooooootiating' because of his constant use of these two words, which would usually be delivered in a sort of monotone, along with his lectures.

There were plenty of enjoyable moments too, as the following photographs illustrate. They are all reproduced by kind permission of Frank Brewitt, a Lancashire Constabulary recruit, who began his training at Bruche on 31st May 1948. The first photograph is of Frank's class, he is third from the right on the front row.

The following photograph shows Frank and his colleagues in various modes of dress, which would probably all have been worn at various stages of their training (and leisure hours!)

The next two photographs appear to show Frank and his friends taking their role very seriously, and getting in some practical training sessions after their day's work in class. They have made good use of various items of machinery to illustrate two types of incident that a police constable may be expected to deal with. Explanatory titles have been provided by Frank!

'Speeding Offence'
The penalty being exacted from the unfortunate motorist for this offence in 1948 appears to have been much more severe than the Fixed Penalty fine that is so common today!

'Road Traffic Accident'

If the casualty in this 'accident' has indeed been injured under the heavy roller, he may well have looked much like Tom in the famous Tom & Jerry cartoons after he has been flattened by something similar!

George Briggs remembers that there were regular cross country runs, where recruits would run out of the centre for a set distance, and then back again. He and some of his colleagues would run as far as the local off licence, where they would stop, and hide in the bushes and have a cigarette before joining in with the rest of the recruits on their return run to the centre.

Recruits returning to centre after a cross country run

The discipline on centre was very rigid, and typical of military discipline, which was what most of the recruits were used to, having come direct from the forces. One of the officers responsible for instructing the recruits in drill, turnout and physical training at this time was Sergeant Williams, from Rochdale, who had formerly been a drill sergeant in the Grenadier Guards.

Security at the centre overnight was carried out by a Constable and a Sergeant, who worked on the gates. If this security duty involved weekend work, then the Constable would be confined to the Centre over the weekend, with no opportunity to visit the hostelries of Warrington during the evening.

George Briggs recalls that a more accurate description of security duty would be that the Constable would be the one who walked round the centre doing the security checks while the sergeant sat in the office!

Entertainment was fairly limited, and usually consisted of walking to the pubs in the area, or having a drink in the centre, or using the billiards room or library.

However, a dance (the first of many which were to follow over the next 60 years) was arranged for the new recruits during the first course, to which many of the local girls were invited.

Dancing in the assembly hall

Following high spirits at the dance, and what has been described as 'a bit of a shambles' with recruits climbing back into the centre over the fence after the curfew, the Commandant was forced to speak to the intake, and reprimand everyone.

Returning to centre after the curfew seems to have been quite a common occurrence. Recruits would come in over the back fence, and dodge the duty officer on many occasions, having spent too long in the pubs of Warrington.

If they were caught, they would be paraded before the Commandant and reprimanded, as they were if they broke any of the rules of the centre.

However, as Derrick Hibberd (F Class, Course 8) who began his training at Bruche on 13th May 1946 told me, the majority of the recruits were ex-services personnel with plenty of experience of dodging 'red caps', so not many were caught.

Cyril Mills recalls how he brought a portable gramophone to the centre, which he would play in the accommodation block while everyone was washing and dressing in the mornings. At this time, radios were not supposed to be played on centre.

The Deputy Commandant, (Mr. Hegg) came into the block one day and asked if anyone in there had a radio. No-one answered. He then asked if anyone had a gramophone, and Cyril duly answered that he had. The Deputy seemed a little put out at the fact that Cyril hadn't answered when he asked about the radio, and stomped off, instructing them not to play it before 8am.

The Deputy Commandant, who hailed from the Liverpool City force, appears to have had a reputation among the recruits on the first course of constantly trying to catch them out.

A good example of how he was outwitted on several occasions was recalled by Cyril Mills.

Recruits left the centre at 1pm on a Saturday, and had to be back by 10pm on Sunday. Cyril and others would come back from Liverpool to Padgate by train on a Sunday evening, which did not leave them much time to get back to Bruche before the 10pm deadline.

At this time, there were still a large number of RAF and Army personnel using the trains, so the police recruits would get the military personnel in the back carriages of the train to stand up against the doors and windows to make it look as if those carriages were packed full. They would leave the front carriage, which would then seem as if it was the only one with any room in it.

Mr. Hegg would then get into the front carriage for the journey, and when the train stopped at Padgate station, that carriage would be the furthest from the station exit, so he would have further to walk to get out, thus allowing the recruits time to get to Bruche ahead of him.

This ploy appears to have worked very well, as none of the Liverpool recruits who travelled by train at that time were caught in breach of the Sunday curfew!

A quotation displayed in the Commandant's office set the standard that was expected of the police recruits, and read;

"Everything that can heighten, in any degree, the responsibility of the office of constable adds to the security of the State and to the safety of the life and property of every individual".

Commandant Seward hard at work in the Commandant's office 1959

First Parade

The first parade of recruits took place at Bruche on 26th April 1946. Of the 305 recruits on parade, 92 had completed their training, and 118 were inspected by Her Majesty's Inspector of Constabulary, Major M. J. Egan OBE.

Among the dignitaries present were Mr. P. Allen, a representative from the Home Office, Captain T. Rawson, Inspector of Police Training Establishments and a number of Chief Constables, chairmen and members of Watch Committees in the area.

Full ceremonial drill was carried out after the inspection and the band of the South Lancashire Regiment played appropriate music.

At the conclusion of the inspection, Major Egan addressed the recruits, and a vote of thanks to him was proposed by the head recruit of the course, Constable R. Walker from Cumberland and Westmorland.

PC Walker paid tribute also to the staff of the centre, chief constables and local authorities. On behalf of the recruits, PC Walker said how much they had appreciated the syllabus and accommodation generally, and they realised the responsibility which attached to them as members of the police forces of the future. He also said that they hoped, by their service to the public, to show that the new system of training would be a successful one.

The vote of thanks was seconded by Constable C. Elliott from Liverpool City Police, who represented the physical training side of the curriculum.

Certificates were then presented to class champions and to class members who had made the most progress.

72 of the 92 recruits who had completed their training had taken life-saving examinations and 70 had passed them. Life-saving awards gained included 20 Elementary Certificates, 3 Intermediate Certificates, 36 Bronze Medallions, 1 Bar to the Bronze Medallion, and 4 Instructors Certificates. It was also noted that approximately half of these men could not swim when they joined the Centre 3 months ago.

Following the presentations, all adjourned to the Assembly Hall where 24 of the recruits gave a display of Physical Training, all of the exercises were performed without verbal commands, and the display ended with a tableau, which was described as 'most effective'.

The drill and PT displays were under the instruction of Sergeant C. Ward, and instructors on parade included Inspector Hodgson from 'A' Class, Inspector Hunt from 'B' Class, Inspector Longcake from 'C' Class and Inspector Archer from 'D' Class.

Although I have not been able to trace any photographs of the PT displays on this first passing out parade, I have included two photographs of PT displays from a passing out parade on 29th July 1948, to illustrate the type of display that would have taken place, albeit out of doors on this occasion.

Vaulting display (29th July 1948) - recruits from E and F classes

Recruits from E and F classes running onto the parade square to begin their PT display (29th July 1948)

Norman Flower was in Class G1, on the 20th course since the opening of Bruche as a police training centre. The course ran from 11.11.46 to 15.2.47. Below is his class photograph, where he is in the centre on the back row.

Norman's uniform had not yet arrived, and his choice of polo necked jumper as alternative dress earned him the nickname 'The Convict'.

The class instructor, seated centre front in the photograph was Inspector Rathbone, from Stockport Borough police.

G1 Class, Course 20

Norman confesses to having trouble settling down after serving in the Army during the war, and that being in a classroom all day did not suit him. To alleviate some of the effects of the classroom, he would wait until the instructor left the room, and draw cartoons of various subjects and happenings during the day. He signed these 'Dragon' and always managed to be back in his seat before the instructor returned.

At first, the instructor just rubbed the drawings out, but as they continued to appear, he started to demand that the person responsible should stand up. This did not work either, and the identity of the artist remained a mystery to him for some time.

However, one day Norman was busy drawing on the board, accompanied by various ribald remarks from among his class colleagues, when he noticed that they had fallen silent.

Turning round, he could not immediately see the reason for the sudden silence, but then a voice from his seat in the class said 'So you are the Dragon?' The inspector had returned, unnoticed by the artist, and was seated in his chair among the class.

Norman was forced to admit that he was indeed 'Dragon', at which point the instructor replied, 'Then I must play St. George!' Fortunately, St. George did not slay the Dragon on this occasion, and Constable Flower was able to leave Bruche and continue his police service with the Manchester City force.

Jim Stowers, (E. J. E. Stowers, QPM) who joined the Devon Constabulary as Constable 314 in September 1949, was sworn in as a constable, together with 2 other new Devon recruits before a magistrate in the main hall of Exeter Guildhall. They were kitted out and given rail tickets to Warrington, and instructed to go to Bruche.

After a long train journey, the three arrived in Warrington in the evening, and were met by a civilian driver, who loaded their suitcases into a station wagon, and drove them to Bruche.
After he had done this, and unloaded their cases at Bruche, they all chipped in 2d, and gave him a total of 6d for his trouble.

The following day, along with the other new recruits, they paraded in uniform to be inspected, and to receive the customary welcome speech, by the Commandant, Mr. Hawkins. Imagine Jim and his two friends' surprise when they realised that the Commandant had been their driver of the night before – especially when they tried to remember what they had said on their journey with him!

Fortunately the incident did not have a detrimental effect on their careers, as they all made their passing out parade, where they were inspected by James Chuter-Ede, who was then Home Secretary.

Mr. Chuter-Ede stopped in front of Jim, and asked him who the clothing contractors that had provided his uniform were. Jim hadn't a clue, so he replied "A tailor's firm in London". This seemed to satisfy Mr. Chuter-Ede, and he moved on. Strange question, Jim thought, and an even stranger answer!

However, having looked at the next photographs, which show the Home Secretary at Jim's pass out parade, I think he may have been looking for a tailor to make him some new, longer trousers!

The Home Secretary, Mr. J. Chuter-Ede at pass out parade in September 1949. The Commandant, Percy Hawkins is standing next to the seated man with glasses

Mr. Chuter-Ede inspects the recruits

Women Officers at Bruche in the 1940s

The first women recruits were sent to Bruche in April 1946, on the seventh course there. There were a total of twelve women on this course, with 3 in A Class, 3 in B Class, 2 in C Class and 4 in D Class. I have been unable to trace any of these first policewomen, but the 4 class photographs are reproduced here.

A Class Course 7- 29.4.46 to 29.7.46

B Class Course 7- 29.4.46 to 29.7.46

C Class Course 7- 29.4.46 to 29.7.46

D Class Course 7- 29.4.46 to 29.7.46

The first policewoman I have traced during my research into policewomen at Bruche is Jenny Kewley (nee Dobson), who was a member of the Blackpool Borough force, which she joined in June 1946. She went to Bruche on 17th June 1946, and is pictured seated fifth from the right on the front row of the photograph below.

K Class Course 10 – 17.6.46 to 14.9.46

Jenny had worked with the Lancashire force as an auxiliary during the war until April 1946, when the auxiliaries were disbanded. She then applied to join the Blackpool Borough Police, and was accepted as PW 1, the first regular policewoman to join the Blackpool force. She was a guest at the final pass out parade at Bruche on 26th May 2006.

Jenny recalls the accommodation for women at Bruche was completely separate from the male accommodation, and was divided into individual rooms, one for each woman. The central area of the accommodation block had a kitchen, where the women could make tea.

Sometimes the women would make tea in their accommodation block and pass it out through the window to male colleagues outside, as males were forbidden from entering the female block.

Another of the early policewomen to attend Bruche, Dorothy Dixon, was featured in her local newspaper, the Westmoreland Gazette, published on 23rd April 1949. The Gazette reported the fact that Dorothy was the first policewoman to be recruited to the Cumberland and Westmoreland Constabulary. An extract from the Gazette report follows:

'County's first Police Woman

Lakeland recruit to start at Kendal

Formerly a van driver in Kendal, 27 year old Miss Dorothy May Dixon of Ambleside will on Monday morning become Westmorland's first policewoman. Miss Dixon who was accepted for the Cumberland and Westmorland Constabulary nearly four months ago is now completing the final week of her three months training at Bruche Police Training College. She will be stationed at Kendal.

Miss Dixon who weighs just over 11 stone and is 5ft 8 inches in height is maintaining a family link by joining the police service. Her grandfather the late Mr. James Wrennall was a Constable at Dalton in Furness.

This appointment comes after several long debates on the question of women police by Westmorland Standing Joint Committee. Others are to be appointed, two in Westmorland and the same number in Cumberland. Miss Dixon's number is "PW.2". The numeral "PW.1" is being reserved for a woman sergeant who will be stationed at the County police headquarters at Penrith.

Sadly, Dorothy is no longer alive; however she is pictured in her class photograph on the opposite page, seated second from the right on the front row.

Recruits on their way into Bruche 1959

Recruits arrive at Reception 1959 – theatre building on the left

Bill Waller's class at Bruche (March 1950)

Bill Waller of Lancashire Constabulary, pictured far right on the back row, remembers that daily life at Bruche in 1950 included lots of drill practice, both for marching drill and traffic control drills.

Drill practice on the Parade Square 1959

Policewomen's drill practice on the Parade Square

Drill Instructors at Bruche through the years have acquired quite a reputation, with names such as 'The Screaming Skull', and 'The Rochdale Screamer' being attached to them (although probably not to their faces!)

Recruits would be in constant fear of attracting the attention of one of these fearsome men, who would scream and bark insults and instructions at them for the slightest misdemeanour.

One recruit in the 1950s arrived in full 'Teddy Boy' regalia, with drainpipe trousers, drape jacket, shoe string tie and crepe soled shoes. He was met by the drill instructor, who barked out instructions to get back home and come back the next day looking like he wanted to be a policeman. I am reliably informed that the unfortunate recruit did just that!

Another incident occurred on an extremely cold day in 1951, when the Physical Training Instructor had taken the male members of a class of recruits on a cross country run.

Feeling sorry for the female recruits in the cold weather, he had instructed them to stay behind in the gym, which was in one of the old army buildings like the one in the photograph on the previous page.

The girls did so, but curiosity overcame them, and they opened the door to watch another class doing drill practice on the parade square.

This was to prove to be their undoing, for they were spotted by the drill instructor, who ordered them out on to the square and made them join in the drill practice, wearing only their shorts and vests.

However, the drill instructor showed that he was human after all, when, at the end of the course he told the girls that he had to be hard on them, as they were going out into a very rough world and he was trying to prepare them for that.

Snow clearing on the parade square 1958

Sometimes the drill instructors would also be PTIs, and teach recruits about unarmed combat. This sometimes took the form of the instructor pushing or hitting the recruit, barking at them to 'Defend yourself then – hit me back!' or words to that effect (possibly more colourful than can be repeated here!)

On one occasion, there was a recruit in the class who had been a boxer, and he was rather reluctant to hit the instructor when told to do so. He protested that he didn't want to hit him, but the instructor persisted, saying 'Go on son, you won't get through my defences'.

Unfortunately for the instructor, the recruit did manage to get through his defences and hit him, knocking him out cold.

He was carried out of the gym on a stretcher, much to the glee of the other recruits, some of whom had been found wanting on his parade that morning for undone buttons, or long hair etc. and who had been screamed at in front of their colleagues for their misdemeanours.

Fortunately the instructor was not seriously injured, although he suffered a severe blow to his pride, and no doubt the embarrassment did nothing to temper his screaming and barking of insults on the parade square.

Drill instructors were also responsible for getting recruits up to the standard required for their passing out parade, and usually managed it very well, despite some of the recruits never having marched before in their lives.

Dennis Wood recalls how, in the days before advanced sound systems, the music for passing out parades was provided by old 78 records and a gramophone, linked to loudspeakers.

Someone would be tasked with the responsibility of putting the needle on the record and lifting it off again at the right time.

The most difficult bit of this performance was during the 'Advance in Review Order', when the parade would march forward for 14 paces and come to a halt in front of the Inspecting Officer's dais (commonly called 14 One Two – 14 paces and the One Two being the Halt). It necessitated the unfortunate person having to put the needle on the record at just the right moment for the parade to begin to move and lift it off as soon as they had halted.

No doubt much fear was in the heart of the gramophone operator at the thought of the 'advice' he would receive from the drill instructor if he got it wrong on the day!

In fact, Paul Burton, who was an instructor at Bruche in the late 1960s recalled how he and a colleague, Ted Knipe were tasked with providing music at the right moment during a passing out parade.

Normally, this would be done from a small room on the roof of the building adjacent to the parade square, where the operator had a clear view of what was happening, and so knew exactly when to put the music on by placing the needle on the record.

Unfortunately, on this occasion, the record player and its operator, Ted, were stationed in the ladies toilets, on the ground floor below the observation post, occupied by Paul, so Ted had to rely on Paul to indicate by waving when to put the record on.

The ladies toilets were rather dark, and at the point in the parade when the order was given for 'General Salute' Paul waved to Ted to put the music on, which he duly did.

However, due to the lack of light he managed to put the wrong record on, and the assembled dignitaries, guests and recruits on parade were regaled with the first few bars of 'Tiger Rag', which caused much consternation and hilarity.

The drill instructor was extremely annoyed, and thought they had done it deliberately, and they were forbidden from ever doing the music at pass out parades again!

In the next photograph, an unfortunate recruit is receiving some 'advice' from a drill instructor, who appears to be trying to prepare him for the very rough world he is going out into!

During the 1950s, the then Home Secretary, Richard Austen Butler was the reviewing officer for a Passing Out parade at Bruche, and he is pictured in the next photograph, inspecting some of the members of staff on the parade.

This photograph was kindly provided by Sergeant Stan Freestone, a swimming instructor, who is 3rd from the right in the picture.

The Home Secretary inspects some of the staff

On 6th February 1952, King George VI died at Sandringham, and his State funeral took place on the 15th February 1952 at Gt. George's Chapel in Windsor Castle.

Lessons were temporarily suspended while the funeral was conducted. All the recruits at Bruche at the time were lined up in their classes, and joined by members of the instructional staff on the Parade Square during the funeral, which was relayed live from the wireless via loudspeakers to the parade.

Sheila Simpson from the East Riding Constabulary remembers that it was a very cold, grey, February day, and that they seemed to be standing on the parade square for hours. Everyone was glad to be able to begin to march off, so as to get their circulation going again.

During the 1950s, there was a requirement to 'parade' for dinner in an evening. Recruits were expected to be in the dining room a few minutes before the Commandant, and were not allowed to sit down until the Commandant had entered and sat down in his place.

Commandant and staff were on a top table with all the students in columns down from the top table. There was a formal dress code and the Commandant told the recruits when to sit down and when to start eating etc. The person at the end of each table was responsible for serving the food to the others on that table.

Recruits in the dining room 1959

Sheila Simpson recalls that during the afternoon tea break, dry teacakes (with no butter) were served. After several weeks, the recruits were sick of these dry offerings, so Sheila and her classmates took some back to class with them, and placed them all in the instructor's desk, closing the lid on them. The desk was very high, and the instructor would always walk into class, lift up the lid of his desk and place his hat inside, then closing the lid.

She recalls that, on this occasion he walked in, opened the lid, never flinched, and placed his hat at the side of the room, continuing with the lesson as if nothing had happened!

Bruche in the 1950s still had accommodation in the old huts, which can be seen in the photograph which follows, taken on a snowy day in February 1958.

I Block is the block at the front of the photograph

Bert Ellis and Ron Sonerson, two of the drivers who drove the bus at Bruche, pictured with an 'icy' friend in February 1958

In the late 1950s, a new classroom and teaching building was erected, this would be the first building to the left of the entrance, and it was still in use as a teaching block until the centre closed in 2006.

It is an 'L' shaped building, in two storeys, and has been primarily used as a teaching block over the years. It incorporates a gym, where personal safety and fitness training took place.

Classroom block, with the gym building at the end of the footpath 1961

Classroom Block 1961

There have also been various offices located in this building, as well as classrooms, from time to time, including an Inspectors office, trainers' workroom and other offices.

In 2006 it housed the trainers' team workrooms, team leaders' office, specialist trainers' office, gym, file checking unit, interview training rooms, and classrooms.

In the photograph below, which shows recruits in the canteen in 1959, you can clearly see through the windows that the new teaching block is under construction.

Some of the kitchen staff, pictured in 1958

Classes ended at 12 noon on Saturday, when recruits were permitted to leave the centre, but they had to be back by 10.30pm on the Sunday, ready to begin classes again on the Monday morning.

Teaching was still very formal, and the recruits sat in rows at desks, while the instructor stood at the front. Bill Waller remembers having to copy down lots of legislation in a foolscap exercise book, which was supplied to all recruits for the purpose. Recruits were expected to learn definitions of offences, laws, vehicles and many more. There would be regular checks to see if they had learned their definitions, recruits would be regularly asked to repeat a definition for the instructor and heaven help them if they couldn't do so!

Bill also recalls that there were regular exams, but he can't remember how often and that officers who failed just one exam were returned to force and presumably sacked.

Power of Arrest lesson

Discipline during the 1950s was still very strict, and I have had reliable information from several recruits who were at the centre during this period that the Commandant (Mr. Hawkins) would patrol the centre with a lamp at night, to make sure everyone was in their accommodation when they should be.

A favourite haunt of recruits on a Wednesday evening was a club in Warrington town centre. Apparently there were two clubs opposite each other, and the other one was frequented by American Service personnel from Burtonwood Air Base nearby.

Recruits enjoy a drink in the bar 1959

Albert Short, who was a Wigan Borough officer, was at Bruche during May, June and July 1958.

Albert very kindly provided me with the first of his 'neat books' which he completed during his time at Bruche.

The 'neat book' was required to be completed in the evening, after day classes had finished, and contained details of the information given during the day's lessons.

The lesson 'Aids to Study' informed the student that 'WRITING IS A GREAT AID TO MEMORY'. It was thought that the taking of rough notes during lessons, followed by the writing of the 'neat book' would assist students to retain the information.

The 'Rules for the Writing of the Neat Book' were as follows:

Rule 1: Each lesson must be written in ink
Rule 2: The lesson must be copied exactly
Rule 3: Work through the book from left to right
Rule 4: Start each new lesson at the top of a fresh page
Rule 5: Include the title of the lesson, the number, and underline it
Rule 6: The writing must keep abreast of the weekly work
Rule 7: Charts must be recorded in ink starting at the back of the book
Rule 8: Any queries regarding alterations etc. in the précis see the class instructor
Rule 9: Leave an inch and a quarter margin on the left of each page

Albert's 'neat book' contains much information about the lessons he studied whilst at Bruche, including the following instructions on how to patrol a beat:

a) *By day a constable should make himself conspicuous, walking on the edge of the pavement, be ready to answer any questions, observe the people, search for wanted persons, maintain a traffic flow, and help the elderly and infirm to cross the road.*

b) *By night when the streets have cleared, he should walk on the inside of the pavement, giving special attention to the security of premises, the prevention and detection of crime or outbreaks of fire, and preventing nuisances.*

Other subjects covered in Albert's 'neat book' included:

The Historical Development of the English Police System, Organisation of a Police Force, Police Acts and Regulations, Police Communications, how to complete the officers' notebook, Common and Statute Law, Evidence, Care, Custody, search and charge of prisoners, Courts, Animals, Warrants, Summonses, Lost and Found Property, Missing and Destitute Persons, Road Accidents, and many others including lots of legislation relating to the use of motor vehicles.

The lesson entitled 'Animals – Common Terms, Straying, Ill or Injured' informed the students that *'The colour or the points of a horse, or its harness, may have to be described more frequently than the details of any other animal'* and that a chart showing particulars of the points and the various items of harness was exhibited in the Training Centre.

Recommended reading for the students at the time included the following:
The Police of Britain by S. F. Moylan – Price 1 shilling
Short History of the British Police by C. Reith – Price 3s 6d
Police Procedure and Administration by C.C.H Moriarty – Price 10 shillings

Students were advised that text books were *'a valuable possession'*, and to concentrate at first on Moriarty's Police Law, as *'it is full of interest'*. Students were also instructed to read one of the police periodicals regularly, the weekly Police Review or Police Chronicle, and the quarterly Police Journal.

Students in class 1959 – the absence of text books suggests that they are having some sort of exam or test

Recruits were taken to Warrington Baths to learn swimming and lifesaving. Audrey Oglanby from Lancashire Constabulary recalls that, when she did her training at Bruche in 1959, they were transported to the baths in the back of an old army type covered truck – not exactly the most comfortable form of transport!

The recruits in the photograph below are about to board a slightly more up-to-date mode of transport to take them to Warrington Baths.

Recruits board a bus to Warrington Baths 1959

Bus driver Paddy Doherty and the Bruche bus - 1958

Arriving at Warrington Baths 1961-2

A class of recruits at Warrington Baths in 1959

Sheila Simpson has a vivid memory of being involved in a swimming lesson at Warrington baths one day when the building was struck by lightening. She recalls being particularly concerned about some of the poorer swimmers who were holding on to the metal bar that ran around the baths at the time.

Some panic ensued, and the building was evacuated, but fortunately no-one was injured and everyone was given hot, sweet tea to help them recover.

Learning to swim at Warrington Baths in 1959

The photographs that follow show recruits in the 1950s being taught first aid, a certificate in which was an obligatory qualification for police recruits.

Sgt. Inman (Blackburn Borough) teaching first aid - 1959

Sport at Bruche

One of the more unsavoury sporting incidents which happened at Bruche in the 1950s was recalled by David Mitchell.

David was a qualified football referee, and went to referee the Bruche football team game against St. Helens, which was played at St. Helens.

He remembers that one of the recruits from the Bruche team was much later out of the dressing room than the rest of the team, but thought no more about it, being anxious to get the game started.

At the end of the match, the teams retired to their dressing rooms, only to discover that all the cash from everyone's pockets had been stolen, along with 2 postal orders worth £14 which were 'demob' money from the RAF belonging to one of the recruits.

No-one was traced as responsible at the time, however several weeks later, the culprit was arrested in Liverpool after cashing in the 'demob' postal orders, and was found to have been a member of the Bruche recruit team.

It was the one who had left the dressing rooms later than the others. He was sacked from the force immediately, and on appearing at court was sentenced to 3 months imprisonment.

Sport at Bruche was encouraged, with recruits joining teams for football and rugby among other sports. Cross country runs were still undertaken (with many ways of avoiding them, or shortening the distance still being carried out!), and there were boxing tournaments, netball, snooker and darts on offer out of classroom hours.

Bruche Rugby Team 1958

Bruche rugby team in action 1959

Netball practice

Vaulting instruction in PE class

Boxing winner 1959

Memories of Bruche – Sir James Anderton CBE, QPM, DL

Former Chief Constable of Greater Manchester Police

'Clutching my ration book and a few personal possessions I arrived at Bruche for the very first time on a miserably wet Monday morning on 30th March 1953, to begin my career as Constable D52 of the Manchester City Police.

The place had the distinct aura of a barracks; thankfully not forbidding for those like me who had already served in the armed forces, as regulars or national servicemen, well accustomed to strict discipline, rigorous physical training, drill parades, and the privations as well as the benefits of communal life.

It was still a time of austerity following the Second World War and we felt sufficiently well rewarded as probationer constables on a salary of £400 a year.

Our intake was the 140th recruits course – an indication of the thousands of recruits who had passed through the Centre since it was opened. My class comprised eighteen members; nine from Manchester (including four females), eight from Liverpool, and one from Salford, all from city police forces. There were relatively few women officers in those days, but they were the equal of their male colleagues and in no sense overawed by being outnumbered.

My most enduring memory is the great camaraderie and esprit de corps, the good natured inter-force rivalry, and the mutual support we gave each other throughout the course, whether in the classroom or on the sports field.

I remember too, the pride and passion of our passing out parade on Friday 27th June 1953.

On the eve of my retirement, exactly thirty eight years later, on Friday 28th June 1991, I was privileged to attend my final parade at Bruche as the day's Inspecting Officer, and publicly acknowledge that my police career had ended where it all began'.

Memories of Bruche – John Savident

Actor and former Constable with Manchester City Police

John went to Bruche for his initial training on 5th October 1956, as Constable C 88 of the Manchester City Police.

He remembers finishing among the lower achievers in the exams, in fact he thinks he was fourth from bottom of his class. This was no doubt due to him spending much of his spare time directing and producing a revue instead of studying.

John obtained a copy of a score and some published sketches from West End revues, and directed various recruits and staff members in a full scale revue which was performed at the end of their course.

Among the items on the programme were songs from Flanders and Swann, who performed one of the biggest hit shows of the 1950s.

They performed many humorous songs, among them one called Terribly House and Garden, which was performed in the Bruche revue.

John also recalls that recruits on his intake managed to get one of the cars that were used for role plays into the main doors of reception, blocking the entrance completely, much to the annoyance of the staff.

The Commandant of the time had a lawn, which was his pride and joy, outside the French windows of his house.

Imagine his horror when he discovered the parting gift left on his lawn by recruits from John's intake, who carefully wrote out a message to him in weedkiller, to be discovered after they were long gone. The message read 'F*** off!'

Station 'X'

The Veteran's Memorial at Kelly Air Force Base

The memorial brick at Kelly AFB to all who served at Station 'X'

Joan Douglas (seated) with her Imperial Service Medal. Donald Lodge (former Head Chef) and Audrey Ballatti (former member of housekeeping staff) are also pictured.

The Duke of Westminster presents an award to a student at an Intake Dining - In circa 1980

Superintendent Peter Kinson introduces Mr. McLean to Dave Griffiths, Officer in charge of the Golden Jubilee Parade in 1996

Bruche tradition - recruits throw their hats in the air at the end of the Golden Jubilee Parade 1996

Public Order Training 1996

Swimming Instruction in the Bruche pool

Aerial view of Bruche 2004

Charity at Bruche

Special Agent A. Lance Emory from the US Consulate receives a cheque for £10,000 raised by staff & students at Bruche for the families of the police officers killed in the attack on the World Trade Centre in 2001

Female staff from Bruche who ran the Cancer Research Race for Life to raise money for breast cancer research, in memory of Linda Noguerol, catering manager at Bruche who died from breast cancer in 2001.

Students take part in a charity aerobics session (2001) in aid of the Starlight Childrens Foundation, which grants wishes for sick and terminally ill children. Some students completed the event in public order clothing!

'Bruche'

A Guide Dogs for the Blind puppy, sponsored by Bruche in 2006
The name of Bruche lives on!

Recruits dealing with a role play on Community Involvement Day. Volunteer members of the public came to Bruche for Community Involvement Day, to role play various scenarios for the recruits to deal with.
Community Involvement Day would be near the end of the initial course, and would be the final opportunity to practice on 'live' members of the public before going out to divisions.

Tony Chadwick, a regular volunteer is searched as part of a role play on Community Involvement Day. Tony very rarely missed a Community Involvement Day, and was usually to be found near to the bench outside the classroom block in a stop and search scenario.

Members of the catering staff at Bruche in 2006, just prior to the centre closure. The Head Chef, Phil Richardson is on the left of picture, and had been at Bruche since 1985. Also pictured next to Phil is the longest serving member of his staff, Ray Parkinson, who had worked at Bruche since 1982

Members of the housekeeping staff at Bruche in 2006.
Contrast this picture with the picture of the housekeeping staff in the 1940s, on page 26!

My final pass out at Bruche in March 2003
(Prior to my retirement after 30 years service on 8th April 2003)

Course H 2006 and staff - the final intake at Bruche

Final Parade - 26th May 2006

Final Parade waiting to move off.
The colour party consisted of Dave Griffiths (flag bearer) and escorts Steve Lancashire and Karen Grattage
Dave was the Officer in Charge of the Golden Jubilee Parade in 1996

Bert Gaskin returns the Centre Flag to Dave Griffiths prior to the final march past

Final parade approaches the roundabout prior to the flag lowering ceremony

Final parade waits for the Centre flag to be lowered

Pipe Sergeant Phil McConnell of the Warrington Pipe Band, who played a lament as the Centre flag was lowered for the final time.

Lowering the Centre flag from its place on the flagpole at the centre of the roundabout for the final time.

Flags have been flown from a flagpole on this site since 1942 when the US personnel took up residence, up to 26th May 2006 when the Centre flag was lowered as part of the final parade.

Final Award

PC Amanda Thwaites, Leicestershire Police with her class trainer, PC Kevin Ashworth, GMP.

Amanda was presented with an award at the final parade by one of the VIP guests, former policewoman Jenny Kewley, PW 1 of the Blackpool Borough Police, who trained at Bruche in 1946.

The award will be the final award ever presented at Bruche, and is inscribed:

*'Presented to PC Amanda Thwaites Leicestershire Police
In recognition of the commitment and high standards achieved in the Foundation Training Programme
May 2006'*

Phil Jones addresses the recruits before they are finally dismissed to their duties

In keeping with the Bruche tradition, recruits from the final intake throw their hats in the air at the end of the final parade.

*Some of the last remaining residents at Bruche take a stroll
outside Reception after the centre closed*

1960 – 69

Training at Bruche in the 1960s followed a very similar pattern to the 2 previous decades.
Class work still relied heavily on definitions, all of which had to be learned by heart and which were
tested every month.

The next photograph shows 'L' class from an intake in 1965. The officer at the back of the class with
the towel on his head is Swasie Turner from Liverpool City Police, who had apparently just come from
a swimming lesson!

Roselyn Carey from the Wakefield Police remembers that there were lots of mnemonics to assist
recruits to memorise the endless lists that were to be learned. She also recalls the civil defence
training that recruits received, which included pretending to put out an incendiary bomb with a stirrup
pump! A demonstration of this skill can be seen in the next photograph.

Sergeant Dorothy Bell from Bradford City Police was an instructor at Bruche from 1967 to 1970. She was the first female sergeant to take charge of a class of recruits for the whole of their training at Bruche. Prior to that, female instructors just gave the lessons on sexual offences and chaperoned the female recruits.

Dorothy recalls an occasion when she was taking a class for a practical role play on drunk and disorderly. One of the recruits was chosen to make the arrest of the role player, who, armed with a washing up liquid bottle under his coat, appeared to be relieving himself into the centre fishpond.

As the arresting officer approached the 'offender', he overbalanced and fell into the pond. He stretched out his hand for the officer to help him out – yes, I'm sure you've guessed – and pulled him into the pond with him.

Unfortunately, at this moment, the Commandant walked past, and Dorothy feared the worst. She was surprised when he told her to do what she wanted with the recruits, but not when they were in full police uniform!

Another favourite role play, which has evolved over the years to take into account the developments in motor vehicle technology, was the road traffic accident role play. The photograph below shows a 'driver' surveying the damage to his vehicle prior to being interviewed by the police at the scene.

Drill was still taught to recruits, and drill instructors are legendary figures throughout the history of Bruche. Tony Blackburn, a Lancashire officer remembers that they all seemed to have a set line in patter, which the ex-service personnel had all heard before.

However, sometimes the 'civvies' would laugh at one of the drill sergeant's witticisms, prompting a roar of 'BE QUIET, IT'S ME WHO SHOULD BE LAUGHING!'

Recruits would put on white gloves to be drilled in hand signals for directing traffic. This would inevitably lead to cries of despair from the drill sergeant, which would go something like: 'YOU – YES YOU! YOU ARE IN CONTROL! GIVE A FIRM SIGNAL – YOU'RE NOT WAVING MUMMY BYE BYE! THEY WON'T STOP; THEY'LL BE LAUGHING SO MUCH THEY'LL RUN OVER YOU!' This would be followed by the inevitable: 'STOP LAUGHING!'

Traffic Control drill practice on the parade square

Philip Kitchin from Cheshire Police remembers making the mistake of laughing during a drill session, when he was at Bruche in 1966. His punishment was to stand to attention in the centre of the drill square at 5.00 am the following morning.

It was December at the time, and he was standing to attention as ordered, at 5.00 am , when the drill instructor appeared in his pyjamas and dressing gown, and began feeding the fish in the fishpond.

Having finished feeding the fish, he then dismissed the unfortunate, freezing officer by shouting from the edge of the square, as not being in uniform he would not come onto it!

The cross country runs described in previous years still featured in the 1960s, although the methods of avoiding them developed over time.

Frederick Clare from Warrington Borough recalls how he and two friends dived on the back of a passing tractor and trailer, laden with straw, for a lift around the cross country route. On reaching the back of the centre, they jumped off and jogged in as if they were just finishing the run.

Their big mistake was that they should have waited for the others to return, so it was obvious that they had cheated.

The punishment was to run around the centre running track with full knapsacks on their backs, holding a stick horizontally above their heads until the instructor allowed them to stop.

All this physical training appears to have paid off, as the recruits put on a PT display at their passing out parades.

The next photographs show judo and PE displays by H Class from Intake 333, and their PE display, and were kindly provided for me by Hughie McGuire from Salford City Police.

Judo display – Passing Out Parade August 19

PT Display – Passing Out Parade August 1962

'H' Class Intake 333 march onto the parade square for their PT Display August 1962.

In January 1961, Kevin Broad from Liverpool City Police was at Bruche on his initial training. He recalls an incident that happened during his stay, which resulted in his having to do weekend duty on the centre switchboard.

While he was walking from the classroom to the dining hall, he saw a frog on the grass verge. He trapped the frog under his helmet, and then put it into his pocket. When he got into the dining hall, he put the frog underneath an upturned cup that belonged to one of the female recruits, who was away from the table getting her soup.

On returning to the table, the policewoman lifted the cup to turn it over, and the frog jumped up into the air. Kevin remembers the cup, saucer, bowl of soup and various other items crashing to the floor, as the policewoman screamed. The whole dining room was in uproar, and a sergeant instructor came to see what had happened.

No-one at the table was prepared to 'cough the job', even those who were covered in soup, gravy and other food and drink.

Eventually, Kevin had to own up to save all the people on the table being charged, and received a severe telling off from the Commandant, followed by weekend duty on the switchboard.

Other popular incidents at Bruche included the hoisting of ladies underwear to the top of the flagpole on the roundabout, which seems to have been a common trait across many intakes of recruits over the years.

Neil Smith from the Cheshire Constabulary, who was at Bruche in 1964, recalls a 'Phantom Bugler' who used to play each night after lights out. The phantom was never discovered – maybe he or she is reading this book…..

Neil also remembers being instructed on how to enter smoke filled spaces to effect a rescue.

The instructor was showing the recruits how to enter the roof space of one of the buildings on the centre, which had a metal roof. One of the recruits threw a brick onto the roof, and Neil remembers the instructor coming out like a greyhound from a trap!

Declan O'Carroll from Burnley Borough was an instructor at Bruche from 1966 to 1968. One of the role play sessions they organised at this time was the staging of a mock armed robbery to test the recall of the recruits when describing what had happened. This event occurred on a Thursday when the centre accountant went to the bank by taxi, and returned in the taxi with cash.

Some of the instructors dressed up in boiler suits and balaclavas, and hid near to the accountant's office. Another class instructor lined up the intake on the road just inside the centre. As the accountant got out of the taxi to walk into the office, he was duly ambushed. As he was 'hit' blood appeared to fly out from his head (which was actually from a tomato ketchup soaked ball of cotton wool concealed in the attacker's hand).

This attack took place outside the kitchen, and was witnessed by one of the kitchen staff who promptly fainted, and several recruits got so over-excited that they had to be restrained and reminded that it was only a role play!

Instructors role play an armed robbery in May 1966

On another occasion in the 60s, members of the local judiciary were invited by the Commandant to watch the armed robbery scenario, to see how the recruits could identify (or not!) the perpetrators.

The Commandant kindly offered his car to be used as a vehicle to be ambushed, instructors were to play the parts of the robbers, and Paul Burton, an instructor, was to arrive at the scene driving the ambulance which was used on centre at the time.

The members of the judiciary were assembled outside the admin block, along with several hundred students, to witness the 'robbery'. The 2 perpetrators, dressed in overalls and balaclavas ambushed the victim, and shotgun blasts were heard.

The offenders made good their escape in their vehicle, a Mini Cooper belonging to one of the instructors, out of the front gate and turned right on the main road towards Warrington, before turning right again and back in through the back gate of the centre.

Unfortunately, no-one had informed the local police that this event was to take place, and as the 'getaway' car turned onto the main road, it was seen by 2 police motorcyclists who happened to be passing, and who began to give chase, relaying the information about 2 men in balaclavas as they went.

Reinforcements set off from Warrington Police to assist their motorcyclist colleagues, who had by this time noticed that one of the occupants of the car was carrying a shotgun and relayed this information as well.

Meanwhile, the unfortunate 'victim' lay on the ground, covered in tomato ketchup, awaiting the ambulance to remove him to hospital.

As the Warrington police reinforcements began to converge on Bruche, they were treated to the sight of the ambulance, driven by Paul Burton, making its way to the scene, with it's emergency horns and blue lights on.

Paul meanwhile was blissfully unaware that the brakes weren't all that good on his ambulance, but he was aware of the need to impress both the judiciary and the students.

With air horns 'heehawing' and blue light flashing he sped up towards the victim, applied the brakes, and, in full view of all the recruits and the judiciary members, slid gracefully into the back of the Commandant's car!

As if this embarrassment was not enough, he was then picked out 7 times on a subsequent identification parade as being the driver of the getaway vehicle, which only serves to illustrate to the members of the judiciary that identification is not always reliable, even when it is made by police officers.

Another enjoyable lesson in the 1960s was the civil defence lesson, which aimed to teach the recruits how to carry out their duties in the event of war.

> The next photograph shows a group of recruits from 1961 being briefed on civil defence duties (although the officer at the front of the photograph appears to have lost interest).

Sgt. Inman briefs the recruits for a civil defence lesson

Part of the civil defence duties would have included fire fighting, and in the photograph which follows, an intrepid recruit, having arrived on the motorcycle which can be seen in the background, is obviously on his way to a fire, equipped with a bucket of water.

The photograph below shows some of the group relaxing after their efforts, secure in the knowledge that the country would be safe in their hands in the event of war breaking out!

Of course, all recruits had to be familiar with the use of gas masks, to enable them to breathe while carrying out their duties in times of attacks involving gas. The next photograph shows a group of recruits receiving their gas mask training, outside the classroom block in 1959.

Not all of the training at Bruche was so enjoyable however. Gordon Finney of Bolton Borough Police who was at Bruche in November 1964 vividly recalls the visit he made to the local mortuary. He still remembers seeing the body of a young girl of approximately 6 years old, who had been murdered, and found on waste land near Bruche. The memory of her and of her injuries remains with him to this day.

One event that happened at Bruche in the 1960s, recalled by Sergeant Dorothy Bell, was an unscheduled visit to the centre by Myra Hindley, one of the infamous Moors murderers.

Myra Hindley and Ian Brady were convicted of five murders on 6th May 1966 and jailed for life. Their victims were 16 year old Pauline Reade, 12 year old John Kilbride, 12 year old Keith Bennett, 10 year old Lesley Anne Downey, and 17 year old Edward Evans.

The body of Edward Evans was found at the house Brady and Hindley shared in 1965, and the bodies of Lesley Ann Downey and John Kilbride were found buried on Saddleworth Moor outside Manchester shortly after the body of Edward Evans was discovered.

The body of Pauline Reade was found buried on Saddleworth Moor in 1987, after Hindley was taken from prison to assist in the search. The body of Keith Bennett has never been found to this day.

Hindley was being escorted on her way from prison to visit her dying grandmother, Ellen Maybury, when the driver of the car she was travelling in mistook the Police Training Centre for Risley Remand Centre, a short distance from Bruche. He was duly re-directed to Risley, and went on his way, taking his infamous passenger with him.

During the 1960s and part of the 1970s, prisoners from Appleton Thorn open prison near Warrington were employed in the gardens at Bruche.

The next picture is of Jim Armstrong, from Manchester City Police. If you look carefully, you can see a garden hoe leaning on the sign, just behind and to Jim's right.

The hoe had been left by one of the prisoner/gardeners, who was obviously reluctant to be photographed, as he had made a swift exit when he realised that there was to be some photography taking place!

The photograph below shows some of the staff at Bruche in 1968, with Sgt. Jack Nicholls on the far right of the centre row. Sgt. Nicholls was a drill instructor at Bruche, and the inter-class marching competitions at Bruche were for 'Jack's Plaque', a plaque named after Sgt. Nicholls.

The 1960s also saw the arrival of overseas police officers for training at Bruche. They were trained as CID officers and also as Instructors.

Students on the CID courses came from Ghana, Grenada, Jamaica, Malawi, Malaysia, St. Vincent, Bahamas, Bahrain, Bermuda, Gilbert & Ellis Islands, Hong Kong, Pakistan, Swaziland, and Trinidad.

Students on the Instructors Courses came from Nigeria, Ghana, Lesotho, British Honduras, and Malawi among other places.

Ken Irvine, a former recruit and later instructor at Bruche has kindly provided the following photograph of the overseas students on Overseas Student Instructors Course No. 2 in early 1970.

The officer on the left of the back row is Winston Carcomo, who was an Assistant Chief Constable from British Honduras Police.

Ken recalls that it was unusual for overseas courses to be run at Bruche, they would normally take place at the Police College at Bramshill. However, he says that both staff and students at Bruche went out of their way to welcome the overseas officers into the Bruche family, and that the courses were very enjoyable for all concerned.

Memories of Bruche – Swasie Turner MBE

Former Liverpool City Police, now charity fund raiser extraordinaire, artist, cartoonist and author

I, like thousands of other police officers, attended Bruche in 1965 for my (strict) initial training, which prepared us for the dangers and traumas of patrolling Britain's dangerous streets.

We were taught law to a very high standard, first aid, how to deliver babies (I was to deliver three during my career), unarmed combat and the skills of diplomacy. Each individual officer was instilled with the utmost confidence, enabling them to use his or her own discretion, initiative and common sense when having to deal with any scenario.

Nothing less than strict punctuality and total smartness of turnout were tolerated. Physical fitness and mental agility were also the expected requirements to ensure each police force received 'value for money' from the Bruche regime. These requirements were all taken in the young recruit's stride, and discipline at the centre was extremely strict. At the completion of the course, the end result was a highly trained and professional police officer.

The young officer's ceremonial passing out parade in front of his or her extremely proud relatives and friends, before being posted to their individual police forces was a major event, and a big incentive at the conclusion of their training.

Pass out parade
Thursday 10th June 1965, the big day! After breakfast we all donned our best uniforms. Jock and I gave each other one last meticulous brush down before emerging into the sunlight to go on parade. On the square everyone looked resplendent in their immaculate turnout.

My uniform tunic sleeves and trousers were creased to razor sharp perfection, thickly soaped on the inside so that the wax would hold them stiff, I could almost shave with them. My white cotton gloves were dazzlingly clean, the toe caps of my boots were polished to mirrors.

What a parade it was. I felt so proud, I was almost moved to tears marching to the sound of the band. Everyone had a fabulous day. Each and everyone were so proud of their newly qualified Police Officer friend or relative, who they had come to see at their moment of triumph.

Swasie passing out on 10th June 1965

On one of the saddest days of my life, namely a very windy and extremely wet Friday 26th May 2006, I and hundreds of other equally sad and disbelieving past and serving officers of all ranks attended the establishment's final parade.

I heard many comments of dissent, and even anger, at the decision to close such a well established and efficient academy. The Almighty too showed his own dissent, as the whole morning's meticulously rehearsed parade was to be a total and utter drenching washout.

I personally think that the establishment will one day regret their ridiculous decision to close such an extremely valuable asset to our increasingly crime-ridden country.'

Swasie has very kindly drawn the following cartoon for me to include in the book. I think that, although it's funny, it also illustrates the strength of affection that exists among former staff and students for the Centre, which has played such a major role in many lives.

BRUCHE CLOSURE

For more information about Swasie and his charity fund raising visit his website at

www.swasieturner.org

1970 – 1979

In the 1970s, the modifications and improvements that had been made to the Centre meant that there was now accommodation for 486 students, 426 male and 60 female. There was a mix of 'dormitory' type accommodation and individual accommodation, and the capacity for instructors had increased to 40. There was now no accommodation on the centre that had been built earlier than 1960.

In addition, there was a residential domestic block for members of the civil service staff who were required, or preferred to be residential, and four self contained flats with accommodation for a further 12 residents. In all, the total accommodation capacity was 550.

The people I have spoken to about this period at Bruche recall the 'reception committees' that were operating at the time.

Chris Quirk from the Isle of Man Constabulary remembers that, after arriving at Bruche on the Sunday night for the first time, in the early hours of the following morning the new recruits would be disturbed by a commotion in the corridor of the accommodation, and loud knocking on everyone's doors.

On looking out to see what the panic was about, the somewhat sleepy recruit would be met by a number of uniformed sergeants and inspectors. The recruits were all made to stand to attention in the corridor and then inspected. If their pyjamas were 'the wrong colour' or their hair was 'too long' they were ordered into PE kit, and told to run several laps of the running track.

It was only later in the day, when other recruits who were a bit longer in service could be seen about the centre that they were recognised as the sergeants and inspectors from the early hours of the morning, and the new recruit realised that they had been had.

Apparently, all the instructors would refuse permission for their uniforms to be used for this practice, but would leave them hanging in a convenient place so that the perpetrators could easily access them.

Needless to say, these new recruits went on to repeat the deception on the next unfortunate intake!

One of the characters to emerge around this time was the swimming instructor, Sergeant Ernie Storr. Ernie was originally a Salford City officer, then Manchester & Salford and Greater Manchester Police.

Ernie was an ex Marine Commando, who had appeared in the film 'Cockleshell Heroes', and his skill at swimming was legendary. In the 1950s he was a member of the Special Boat Service and a bodyguard for Lord Mountbatten. He also boxed competitively against Randolf Turpin, Britain's first black boxing champion.

He was awarded the BEM for his services to charity, and it is thought that he helped to raise over three quarters of a million pounds for various charities.

Many recruits, including myself have been witnesses to what has been described as Ernie's 'party trick' in the swimming pool.

Ernie would stand at one end of the pool, and light up a cigarette, smoking it until it reduced a little in size. He would then turn the cigarette round, put the whole of it inside his mouth, dive in the pool and swim under water to the other end. He would then get out of the pool, pop the cigarette out of his mouth and continue to smoke it as if nothing unusual had occurred! This trick earned him the nickname of the 'Smoking Dolphin'.

There are many recruits, myself among them, who would not have learned to swim without Ernie, and I would certainly never have managed to learn to swim, and then achieve the Royal Life Saving Bronze Medallion for lifesaving without him.

Ernie died on 25th June 2006, almost exactly a month after Bruche finally closed its doors on 26th May 2006.

During the 1970s, First Aid was still taught, and the Centre had an award winning first aid team, made up of instructors Ian Tootell, George MacDonald, Dave Roberts and Ian Moss. The team would compete at events all over the country, and on one occasion, having come 4th in a competition, the Commandant of the time said that if they ever actually won the trophy he would fill it with drink for them.

Needless to say, this was just the spur that was needed; as the team went on to win a trophy that was described as being 'bigger than the FA Cup'.

Unfortunately, there were a few holes in this trophy, but nothing that a few sticking plasters wouldn't cure. So the Commandant duly joined the team in the bar. The trophy was filled to the brim, at his expense, with a mixture of every drink from behind the bar, and no doubt many sore heads resulted from its emptying!

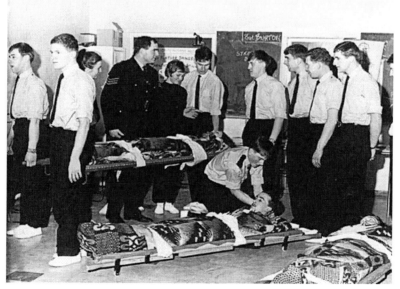

Stretcher drill - Sgt. Paul Burton & recruits 1969

In 1969 – 1970, a new Instructors dining room was built, a new detached house for the Deputy Commandant, a pair of semi-detached houses for staff, and a new suite of offices including a committee room was added as a wing to the administrative block.

In 1972 the swimming pool and all weather football pitch were installed at Bruche, along with the instructors bar. The swimming pool also housed a games hall and changing facilities, and the estimated cost for the pool building when work began in 1970 was £70,000.

The opening of the instructors bar was attended by various Chief Constables of the forces supplying recruits to the centre, and Blaster Bates was the star guest, regaling those present with hilarious tales of blowing things up, which he used to do in the course of his job as a demolition expert.

One former instructor recalls his first day at Bruche, when he decided to visit the instructors bar for refreshment in the evening. Imagine his surprise when he was met by the sight of the Commandant and 2 inspectors playing a game of 'teeth'. This involved them sitting on the floor and throwing their false teeth to see who was the quickest and nearest to the centre of a rose on the carpet. He says he will never forget one of the inspectors dipping his dusty, fluff-ridden teeth into the Commandant's pint of beer to clean them before replacing them in his mouth!

The swimming pool was built near to where the last remaining army hut accommodation block, the old 'L' Block was demolished. This old Block had remained open into the early 1970s, but was finally knocked down to make room for the swimming pool. The next photograph is of the old L Block in 1962, prior to it being demolished in 1970.

Following the opening of the swimming pool, a gala was held, and the next photograph shows the then Chief Constable of Liverpool & Bootle Police, J. Haughton Esq. CBE, QPM, congratulating some of the successful competitors.

Among the many people who have helped me with my research into this book is Donald Lodge, who was head Chef at Bruche from 1978 to 1980.

Kitchen staff at the time included 12 cooks, 6 per shift. All 12 cooks would be on duty at lunchtime, with the early shift and afternoon shift crossing over so as to ensure that enough staff were on duty for the busiest time of the day. There were also 36 waitresses, who worked in two shifts.

The cost allowed for providing a meal for recruits at this time was £1.10p per day, which had to cover breakfast, lunch and dinner, as well as coffee breaks.
The recruits at that time numbered 500, there were 52 instructors, a Deputy Commandant and the Commandant, who all had to be accommodated within this budget.
Donald recalls that the Mayor of Warrington was a regular guest of the Commandant, and he would be invited to lunch or dinner every Thursday.

Donald also remembers making home made soup on at least 4 days a week, which necessitated an enormous amount of preparation of the ingredients to make the 40 gallons of soup that would be consumed by Bruche's hungry residents.

One of Donald's achievements happened one Shrove Tuesday, when he decided that it would be a good idea to serve pancakes to everyone.

Gallons of pancake mixture were duly mixed, and 1100 pancakes prepared, along with over 200 lemons, to be quartered and served with the pancakes. It is reported that the pancakes were enjoyed by the diners, and Donald and his staff's efforts were greatly appreciated.

Another of Donald's ideas was to prepare small cakes for Valentines Day, which again necessitated mixing gallons of cake mixture to make hundreds of cakes. It is not known whether any of the cakes led to romance among the partakers, maybe there is someone out there who could tell us!

Donald left Bruche in 1981, and took up a post as butler to the Marquis and Marchioness of Tavistock at Woburn in Bedfordshire.

The waiting on staff at Bruche at this time were supervised by 2 ladies, Miss May Taylor and Mrs. Joan Douglas, whose husband was later employed as a gardener at the centre.

Joan was awarded the Imperial Service Medal in 1982 for 33 years service with the Home Office at Bruche, along with May Taylor for 36 years, Betty Onions for 26 years, and Marjorie Oxley for 32 years.

There is a picture of Joan holding her medal in the colour photographs section of this book. She is pictured with Donald Lodge and Audrey Ballatti, whose mother-in-law also worked at Bruche for many years from 1948, and is mentioned earlier in this book. All four of the ladies who received the Imperial Service Medal were presented with it at the passing out parade on 1st July 1982.

Joan told me that she had been at Bruche for 23 years, when she and her future husband decided to get married. She remembers being called into the Commandant's office, where she was very touched to learn that he intended to organise her wedding reception on the centre, if she would like him to. It was agreed, and the first wedding reception ever to be held at Bruche was organised and very much enjoyed by the bride, groom and guests.

Over the 60 years it has existed, Bruche has employed many local people, with many of them staying there for years, and with members of their families also working there.

Annie Ballatti, who worked at Bruche from 1948 is known to have still been working there when she was in her 80s, as she was so fond of the place, and her daughter-in-law, Audrey also worked there. All of the people I have interviewed have described working at Bruche as being part of a community, with many saying that it was the best job they ever had.

They say it was such a happy, friendly and warm place to work, with many friendships being formed that have lasted for years. It is very sad to think that such a community is to be broken up and scattered, but I am sure that lots of those friendships made at Bruche will continue for many years to come.

My class of recruits from Intake 440, in 1973. I am second from the right, front row looking like a frightened rabbit!

Daily life at Bruche in the 1970s still included lots of drill practice, for marching, continuity drill, and traffic control drills. Classes of students would compete for the best class in drill, and the winners would be awarded the coveted 'Jack's Plaque', named after a former drill instructor at Bruche, Sgt. Jack Nicholls.

Best uniform, pressed to within an inch of its life, highly bulled boots or shoes, and white gloves were the order of dress for students on a passing out parade.

Those who were no good at uniform pressing, or boots bulling would usually find a volunteer from among the ex-military personnel in their class to either assist with these tasks, or sometimes to do it for them. Generally an offer of a drink or two in the bar would be sufficient encouragement!

Paul Finnegan, who was the Superintendent, Head of Quality at Foundation Training, Centrex at the time of the closure of Bruche in May 2006, clearly remembers his first time on the parade square at Bruche.

It was Monday 28th June 1976, the hottest day on record in the UK. Initially, the recruits were told that they would have to parade in their best uniform, including tunics. However, with a few minutes to spare, they were told that the order of dress would be 'shirt-sleeve order'.

This would have been fine, apart from the fact that Paul had only ironed the collar and 'V' at the front of his shirt, thinking that the rest would be covered by his tunic. I'm sure that he wasn't the first police officer to have used this style of ironing over the years!

Having shared many memories with previous recruits and instructors from Bruche, it seems to have been a common occurrence for at least one person on every intake to have a problem in getting to grips with marching and drill.

There are many stories of 'tick-tocking' (with the arm and leg of the same side going forward at the same time) and also with difficulty in coming to a halt in time with everyone else – rather like Corporal Jones in the TV series Dad's Army.

I remember the attempts made by a class on my own intake to hide a recruit in the middle of the class, in the hope that his marching problems would be made less obvious – needless to say it didn't work!

My Class march off the parade square after their passing out parade in 1973

Teaching in the 1970s was still done in a very formal manner, and the recruits still sat in rows at desks, while the instructor stood at the front.

There were weekly exams, to test student's knowledge, held on a Monday morning. Students who failed these exams would be sent to compulsory evening class on the Monday evening, for extra study.

Male students who visited the centre bar in the evening would be required to wear collar and tie, while females would also have to wear smart clothing. At the end of each evening, after the bar closed, the National Anthem would be played, with all present having to stand to attention while this was done.

All students were expected to be in bed by an appointed time, and the instructor who lived on the block would check all the rooms to ensure that everyone was in bed in their own room before he or she retired for the night. All students had to live on centre during the week, and went home on Friday afternoons until they had to return on Sunday evening.

In early 1971, 'F' Class on a particular intake (which will remain anonymous!) were always in trouble, and eventually their end of intake function was cancelled due to the amount of trouble they had been in. Even the class instructor was unable to get the ban lifted.

However, the Commandant and other members of staff, including an Inspector (described as 'God himself') realised that the recruits would try to get round this ban, and so they carried out several 'raids' on their accommodation to check for alcohol, which was banned. These raids would take place at all hours of the day and night, in an effort to catch the recruits out.

The resourceful recruits managed to overcome the problem of the raids by hiding the crates of beer in the room of a teetotaller from the intake.

The final raid came, and the unfortunate recruit (who had been coerced into hiding the contraband) heard the raiding party of Commandant and Inspector approaching along the corridor.

Several rooms were searched before they finally arrived at his room, and he waited in terrified anticipation of being discovered with the forbidden beer.

As the Commandant and Inspector stood at his door, the Inspector said to the Commandant; "This officer is a teetotaller Sir. "The Commandant looked hard at the recruit before replying; "There won't be anything in this room then" and they both moved on to the next room.

The contraband was never discovered, and was no doubt enjoyed with much relish by the members of 'F' Class (apart from the unfortunate teetotaler).

One instructor in the 1970s was delivering a lesson on how to administer a breathalyser, using the old crystal tube and bag.

The instructor selected a female from the class to drink a mouthful of sherry (which I recall was always of the extremely cheap variety!) so that she could hopefully provide a positive test for all the recruits to see how the crystals changed colour from yellow to green.

Unfortunately this particular recruit had never tasted alcohol before, and reluctantly took a mouthful of sherry and swallowed it. She then promptly threw up all over the classroom floor!

Role plays were still an important part of the curriculum in the 1970s, and a favourite one that was still used was a road traffic accident scenario, which could be varied at the whim of the instructor.

These scenarios would be set up at various places around the centre, and would use instructors' cars, motorcycles or pedal cycles, and the instructors would play the parts of drivers, casualties and witnesses.

The next two photographs show students dealing with a road traffic accident role play in 1973. The accident appears to have involved one vehicle (an Austin Cambridge or a Morris Oxford) colliding with the rear of the VW Beetle at a junction. The students are busy taking notes about the scene, no doubt to help them to fill in the relevant paperwork and reports later.

Students from Intake 440 in 1973 dealing with an accident

The next photograph shows that the accident also involved a pedal cyclist, who appears to have been injured.

Fortunately, in 1973, Bruche was still equipped with the ambulance for use in just such incidents, and this has arrived at the scene.

The unfortunate casualty does not seem to be receiving much attention apart from having his legs securely fastened together with bandages, obviously prior to being removed to the stretcher and onwards to hospital!

The ambulance in the next photograph belonged to the local branch of the St. John's Ambulance Brigade, who parked it at the centre for security.

As a bonus for allowing it to be parked at the centre, it was available for use during role plays, and on occasions it would also be used to ferry some unfortunate soul to hospital, following accidents and injuries at the centre, for example after injuries which occurred during sports sessions.

Students from Intake 440 with the St. John's ambulance

As previously described, recruits knowledge would be tested regularly by exams, which would occasionally produce some strange answers.

It was rumoured at the time that the instructors had a board in their office, on which they used to put 'classic answers' that had been given to exam questions.

One entry from a recruit in 1972 had been asked for the definition of the offence of infanticide. He remembered that the salient points were that the woman had to be suffering from the effects of having given birth, or the effects of lactation.

Unfortunately, he had taken his first aid exam only the previous day, and managed to confidently conclude that it was necessary for the woman to have been suffering from the effects of laceration (instead of lactation) of the breasts!

In 1978 a staff team from Bruche took part in the Chichester RMP March, a 40 kilometre march, under the command of their team leader, the centre Commandant at the time, John Colledge.

The team that took part in this event is pictured in the following photograph, which was kindly provided for me by former Sergeant Pev Smith, who was the first female PTI at Bruche.

The photograph also shows Ernie Storr, the legendary swimming instructor, who is pictured on the second row from the front, on the right.

The centre staff on the Chichester RMP march

In the Commandant's Annual Report in 1978, it was reported that since 1946 when the centre opened as a police training centre, there had been 30,456 male recruits and 5544 female recruits who had completed their initial training there, a total of 36000 recruits in 33 years.

PE was still an important part of the curriculum at Bruche, and the following photographs show recruits in the gym in the early 1970s.

The instructor, right of picture was Sergeant Ted Knipe, known affectionately as Ned Tripe by some of his colleagues.

Recruits in the gym adjacent to the classroom block in the 1960s.

Contrast the previous pictures which date from the 1960s with the one below, taken in the late 1990s. Physical fitness has always been an important part of recruit training, and the facilities at Bruche were improved over the years to accommodate new equipment and training methods.

Recruits in the new gym adjacent to the swimming pool in the 1990s

Wade Dooley England, British Lions 1985 – 93

Bruche Police Training Centre 1976

'May 1976 and following in my old dad's footsteps twenty years earlier, I arrived and enrolled at the Police training centre Bruche as an impressionable, fresh faced 18yr old, and this at the start of what was to be one of the hottest British summers on record.

That was thirty years ago and as retirement from the Lancashire Constabulary looms large for me; I can still look back with clear and fond memories of my ten weeks intensive training at the Warrington police college. Having a father still serving at that time in the Warrington division and being a Warrington lad born & bred you could be forgiven for thinking that I would have had an inkling of life at the college but nothing could be further from the truth.

I found that life at the centre was not too far removed from that of an army recruit, it was extremely disciplined with plenty of early morning drill, bulled boots and classroom law interspersed with the challenges of physical fitness & team building. Weekly written exams honed the senses and concentrated the mind with the threat of 'back classing' for anyone who failed.

The smell of a hot pastry counter still to this day takes me back to the Bruche canteen and morning tea breaks where the raw recruits were treated to cook's sausage rolls which we eagerly devoured dipped in copious amounts of HP sauce.

But life at the college was not all work, following the business of the day we were encouraged to mix and relax in the college bar and many a training centre romance blossomed after last orders in 'Thompson's Grove' which was situated adjacent to the female dorms and unofficially but affectionately renamed over the years as 'Gropers alley' by the students. The weekly 'Ram Sammy's', and final dining in night followed by the passing out parade watched proudly by my family all added to the police college experience.

And the family tradition didn't end there, that very same year I was closely followed through the college by my wife to be, Sharon, a Merseyside Bobby, and four years later my kid brother Paul.

So after an extremely challenging but enjoyable sun drenched ten weeks I departed the training college fitter, wiser and well prepared for a life of policing on the streets of Blackpool and although over the years I never made it back to Bruche, I for one will be sad to see the old place close'.

Wade passing out with his class in 1976

Wade's father looking out of his accommodation block in the 1950s

Memories of Bruche – Tarique Ghaffur, CBE, QPM

Assistant Commissioner, Metropolitan Police

'On the 3ʳᵈ September 1974, I joined Greater Manchester Police and attended Bruche as one of the first officers from a minority community to attend the Police Training Centre.

To me the experience was both intriguing and unusual. In particular I enjoyed some of the humour, camaraderie and all of the sport.

Of course, we were obviously there to learn and academically this was fine; but the sheer volume of material to learn and the weekly exams were tough. However, the discipline of learning has proved useful in my career.

One aspect that I never really came to terms with was the marching. The regimented 'drill and shouting' was alien to both my previous experience and culture. As a consequence, I often found myself out of step with my colleagues, a situation that some commentators would still assert today!

Overall my experience at Bruche, both good and bad, provided me with a strong foundation over the years.

However, I was particularly saddened to watch the recent documentary 'Secret Policeman' and realise that over thirty years on from my time at Bruche, some of the things that should have changed have not in fact done so'.

1980 – 1989

In July 1989, the training system for recruits to the Police Service of England and Wales underwent a radical change.

Following the riots in the early 1980s in Brixton, Moss Side, Toxteth and other areas of the UK, Lord Justice Scarman was appointed to investigate the causes of the riots.

He visited the affected areas and spoke to the police and community. His report highlighted concerns about attitudes displayed by some police officers when dealing with multi-cultural situations.

In order to address these concerns, it became apparent that the training of police officers needed to be re-evaluated to incorporate the social implications of the attitudes and behaviour displayed by police officers.

The University of East Anglia was tasked with carrying out a review of police training, and they recommended a skills-based, modular system of Initial Foundation Training with an emphasis on human awareness, to raise the students' awareness of the potential effects of their attitudes on others.

This system was implemented by all Police Forces throughout England and Wales, and it incorporated a recommended structure of self, peer, trainer and supervisory assessment.

This was based on 36 skills and abilities which were identified in the University of East Anglia's review. These represented what were considered to be the characteristics required by a police officer in a multi-cultural society.

Even with this new system of training, recruits were still expected to learn definitions by heart, and they would still be tested by exams, with extra classes in the evening for those who did not achieve the required standard.

Drill was still part of daily life at Bruche, as were the feared drill sergeants (or drill pigs as they were affectionately known).

One incident recalled by a recruit from the 1980s occurred as he was walking back from a swimming lesson with his hands behind his back. If you were caught with your hands in your pockets, you would have to parade in best uniform at 7am, so it wasn't worth getting caught.

On this occasion, the 'drill pig' was walking in the opposite direction, pace stick under his arm. Upon reaching the unfortunate recruit, he swung the stick round, and poked him in the stomach with it, so that he doubled over in pain.

He then shouted, "WHO THE F****** HELL DO YOU THINK YOU ARE – PRINCE CHARLES?"

The recruit recalls that, from that moment he quickly learned to swing his arms as he walked, so as to avoid further discomfort!

Role plays were still a major part of the curriculum, with instructors playing the parts of various suspects and witnesses.

In the next photograph, taken in 1982 or 1983, students are engaged in a practical session about offensive weapons. Instructors play the parts of the 'suspects', and while one student deals with the scenario, others watch what happens.

Here, the officer is speaking to suspect 1, while in the background suspect 2 (a very suspicious looking individual!) can be seen with a studded belt strapped around his leg and what appears to be a motorcycle chain around his head.

The object of the session was to determine whether the belt or the chain could be classed as offensive weapons or not, and whether the suspect could be arrested.

The class instructor has a clipboard, where he would make notes on the performance of the student, to use in the de-brief of the scenario as to how the student had dealt with it.

The armed robbery scenario would also still be a feature, but the senior intake would be kept in the classroom while the junior intake witnessed the incident. They would then be interviewed by the seniors, and a statement would be taken from them.

The Duke of Westminster (centre) watches a role play in the 1980s

Bruche - the Brookside Connection

In 1987, the 467th episode of Brookside was screened by Channel 4, and featured the Corkhill family attending their son, Rod's passing out parade as a police officer. The parade scenes were filmed at Bruche, and a police adviser to the programme was John Stalker, former Deputy Chief Constable of the Greater Manchester Police.

The photograph below shows, from left to right: Doreen Corkhill (Kate Fitzgerald), Billy Corkhill (John McArdle), Rod Corkhill (Jason Hope), Julia Borgan (Gladys Ambrose), and Rod's girlfriend, Kirsty Brown (Joanne Black).

Brookside photograph produced by kind permission of Brookside Productions Ltd.

Phil Richardson, Head Chef gets a cuddle from Brookside's Julia Brogan, played by actress Gladys Ambrose

Entertainment at Bruche

Entertainment evenings called 'ram samis' were a regular occurrence at Bruche. They were brought in by one of the Commandants, Mr. F. A. Seward.

The 'ram sami' was originally held on a Friday evening, in the theatre. The original reason for this was to keep the officers in the camp, rather than letting them go into Warrington and get drunk, with the potential for causing trouble.

Classes didn't finish until 12noon on Saturdays, and the Commandant thought that a ram sami would solve the problems of late or non-appearance of students in their classes on a Saturday morning.

The ram sami consisted of a show, put on by staff and students, and would include musicians, singers, sketches etc.

Many a talent was discovered at these events, where staff and students would devise and perform a variety of acts for the entertainment of their colleagues.

Below is a photograph of some talented recruits ready to perform in their end of course entertainment show on the 21st August 1952.

Some of the other talent on display at ram samis in the 1950s included Ron Bulmer from Liverpool City force, who played tunes on a carpenter's saw with a violin bow, and Mick Ready, a Physical Training Instructor who had what has been described as 'a fantastic voice'

Some copies of entertainment programmes are reproduced in the following pages.

POLICE TRAINING CENTRE,
BRUCHE,
WARRINGTON

BY KIND PERMISSION OF THE COMMANDANT

ON STAGE AT

8.15 p.m. –TUESDAY 20th OCTOBER, 1970

MIRTH and MAGIC
* * *

MELODY

PRESENTED FOR YOUR ENTERTAINMENT

BY

THE STAFF AND STUDENTS

INTERRUPTED AND INTERFERED WITH BY – SERGEANT PAUL BURTON, I. C. F. A

=1=1=1=1=1=1=1=1=1=1=1=1=1=1=1=1=1=1=1=1=1=1=1=1=1=1=1=1=1=1=1=1=1=1=1=1=1=1=1=1=
1=1=1=
+*+

(1) Excerpt from the show 'Oliver' – with P.W. Belinda Sutton,
Inspector 'Big Al' Moorhouse, Sergeant Jack Nicholls and
Sergeant 'Big Brian' Gregory.

(2)   P. C. Swales entertains, sings and plays guitar.

(3)   "The Fantastic Return of the 14th Week"

Sergeant Nicholls – as Sergeant Benditt
Sergeant Burton - as Inspector Crabshot-Smythe, DSO
P. C. Parsenage   - as P.C. C. C. H. Moriarty

And the rest of 'U' Class

(4)   Music the P. C. Jones way, helped out by his friends.

(5)   "It's a trick!" – Sergeant Thompson baffles us again.

(6)   Hold Tight, Stamp and Clap with 'Big Al' and the Boys and Girls
Singing "The Rhythm of Life".

GOD SAVE THE QUEEN

GOOD EVENING

BRUCHE

GRAND CHRISTMAS SHOW
(BY KIND PERMISSION OF THE COMMANDANT)

Produced By

Jack Nicholls

and

Ron Parkinson

Compere – Jim 'Wallaby' Kerr

1. Carols – Join in with the Bruche Choir.

2. "If I were not upon this Stage".

3. "Dr. I'm in Trouble.

4. Eric Litherland sings accompanied by Stephen Bentley.

5. Problems with "Twenty Tiny Fingers Twenty Tiny Toes".

6. "Three Happy Chappies" – Hugh Thompson, Stephen Ainsworth –
   Joe Belgar

7. "Ma and Pa Kettle" – "Country Style".

8. Malcolm Lee entertains with Guitar and Songs.

9. Jim Hawthorn presents his "Black and White Minstrels".

10. The Warrington Pipe Band

GOD SAVE THE QUEEN

One memorable 'ram sami' performance took place when the Commandant had invited one of Her Majesty's Inspectors of Constabulary and his wife to the evening's entertainment. Also on the front row at the performance were the Commandant, Deputy Commandant, Chief Instructor and their wives.

One of the items on the programme was a performance of the death of Caesar, which contained the famous 'Friends, Romans, Countrymen' speech, to be delivered by a recruit who had trained at RADA as an actor. This particular recruit (who wasn't particularly tall or well built) asked for a volunteer to play the dead Caesar, unfortunately the only one to offer was a strapping 6'2", 17 stone colleague.

Not to be deterred, rehearsals went ahead, and all went well until the night of the actual performance. The RADA recruit and Caesar were both wearing togas; Caesar (with an eye to preserving his modesty) had put on a pair of regulation white football shorts under his toga.

Caesar lay on the stage, on a platform specially erected from pallets, so that he could be seen by the audience, who were seated below the level of the stage. His white toga was stained with blood (well, tomato ketchup!) and he lay motionless as his colleague picked him up, cradling him in his arms and began to deliver the famous speech.

It was at this point that the horrified VIPs on the front row, together with the several hundred recruits sitting behind them began to realise that Caesar's football shorts were rather too baggy to preserve his modesty, which was by now on full view!

The Commandant motioned frantically to one of the instructors who was standing at the side of the stage to do something about it. The instructor decided that the best course of action was to crawl along the front of the stage, behind the footlights area unseen by the audience and to close Caesar's legs for him.

This he did, with a sort of scissor movement but rather too sharply for the unfortunate Caesar, as it caused him some considerable pain.

The audience, who were by now in hysterics, but who couldn't see the instructor, were then treated to the sight of Caesar suddenly coming back to life, sitting up, shouting 'Ow!' and promptly falling out of his colleague's arms onto the floor!

The 'ram sami' entertainment evenings stopped in the 1980s, and entertainment was provided in the form of discos, and the occasional live acts, quiz nights and barbecues in the summer.

A typical Ram Sami performance in the 1960s

This is a song penned by an anonymous instructor author, around the late 1970s about the recruits, who were about to pass out, and was sung to them by the instructors.

WE'VE NOW GOT COPS

(To the tune of 'There is nothing like a Dame')

We had thickies by the score
With their hair down to the floor
They couldn't read or write or swim
They were hopeless in the gym
We'd loungers, loafers, scroungers, flops
Mammies boys and wet milk sops
Now look what we've got
We've now got cops.

There was nothing like a cop
Nothing in the world
There was nothing that we'd got
That looked anything like a cop.

We had ex-cadets and miners
Nurses and precision grinders
We'd Paddies with beer bellies
Who went on the square in wellies
They've had flu and mumps and beri beri
And even one with dysentery
Now look what we've got
We've now got cops.

We had nothing to put on our best gear for
They didn't even know what they were here for
There was nothing like a cop
Nothing in the world
There was nothing that we'd got
That looked anything like a cop.

Now we've genius by the score
Really couldn't ask for more
Ten weeks at Bruche have done the trick
They look so smart and neat and slick
They can do PE, and swim and drill
To see them now gives us a thrill
Now look what we've got
We've now got cops.

This song, parts of which would be deemed inappropriate in the present time, was written to show how much progress had been made by recruits who had come from many different walks of life, and who were now police officers and whose families and instructors were rightly proud of.

Dining-In or Intake Dinners

These took place at the end of each intake's training course, and were very formal, black tie affairs.

Students were expected to dress appropriately; dress code was 'black tie' which meant males in dinner suits and females in long evening dresses.

Tables would be laid out formally, with a top table for staff and guests, and long tables off the top table, one for each class. Seating plans would be allocated for each table, with class instructors at the opposite end from the top table (no doubt to try to ensure that the presence of officers at both ends of the class tables would result in no improper behaviour!).

Students would assemble in the bar for pre-dinner drinks, and at a signal from a member of staff (usually the drill instructor) would move along the long corridor of the administration block to the dining hall.

Ladies would be escorted on the arm of the gentlemen, such arrangements having been decided on before the night, and would be seated opposite one another on the table.

A class from 2001 in the bar before their dining-in

Once all the students were in the dining hall, they would remain standing behind their chairs until the announcement that the Head of Centre and guests were approaching. They would then clap the guests into the dining hall and to their places at the top table.

Grace would then be said, and all would be invited to take their seats, after the top table guests had taken theirs. Proper etiquette would be observed throughout the meal, which would usually consist of six courses.

No-one was allowed to leave the table until after coffee, when the Principal Guest would be asked for permission to call a short break before the prize giving ceremonies began.

At this point there would usually be a mad rush for the exits, probably due to the amount of drink that had been consumed before and during the meal!

Top table at a dining-in in the 1960s

A menu from the Intake Dinner for Intake 422 (my husband's Intake) which was held on Thursday 6th January 1972 is reproduced below:

INTAKE DINNER

Thursday, 6th January 1972

****
***
*

MENU

Prawn Cocktail

Soup

Steak and Onion
Mushroom
Tomato
Creamed Potatoes
Brussels Sprouts
Baby Carrots

Sherry Trifle

Cheese and Biscuits

Coffee

The menu for each dining-in would be devised by the catering staff, and some of the ladies who served food from behind the serving counters normally would don black skirts, white blouses and white aprons and serve the food at the table.

Port would be served in the traditional manner, to the left around the table, with only the gentlemen allowed to touch the decanter. Needless to say, once the equality legislation was passed, this caused much discussion among the male and female students!

Following the meal, the Principal Guest would be invited to present prizes to students, and would give a speech.

One such speech was delivered by Sir James Anderton, then Chief Constable of Greater Manchester Police, during the time of the riots in Moss Side, Manchester in 1981.

Mick Chew, an instructor at the time recalls that all the recruits were terrified because they were about to go out onto the riot torn streets of the country.

He says that Sir James gave an inspiring speech, which left everyone with the belief that they were the best recruits ever. In fact he says it was 'bloody marvellous'!

Dining-in 1978

1990 – 1999

In 1996 Bruche celebrated its Golden Jubilee – 50 years of police training at the centre.

It was decided that various events to celebrate the jubilee would be held, and money raised would be donated to charity. A total of around £16,000 was raised, and donated to the following charities:

Christie Hospital Leukaemia Unit
Niemann-Pick Disease Support Group
North Western Children's Hospices (Derian House & Francis House)

On 19th April 1996, the 50th Anniversary Review parade was held at Bruche. The intake passing out on that date was Intake 9/95, which had a complement of 88 male and 34 female officers. They were drawn from the forces of Cheshire, Greater Manchester, Lancashire, North Wales, Nottinghamshire, Staffordshire, South Yorkshire and West Yorkshire.

The youngest recruit on parade was Constable 732 Melissa Edwards from Staffordshire Police, who was 19 years old at the time.

Parade formed up for inspection 19th April 1996

The Reviewing Officer for the parade was the Rt. Hon. David Maclean MP, Minister of State at the Home Office, who later unveiled a plaque to commemorate the 50 years of police training at Bruche.

Also on parade were police pensioner guests from the original intake in January 1946. They were:

Harold Foulkes, 73 years, from Warrington Borough Police
Albert Gaskin, 74 years, from Manchester City Police
Elfyn Jones, 78 years, Liverpool City Police
Cyril Mills, 72 years, Liverpool City Police
James Peel, 78 years, Cumberland & Westmorland

Principal guests at the parade were:

Sir Trefor Morris, CBE, QPM, CIMgt, HMIC
Mr. Peter Ryan, QPM, MSc, BA, DMS, FIMgt, FIPD, National Director of Police Training
Herr Wolf-Gunter Immisch, Director of Police Training, Federal State of Westfalia, Germany.
(Westfalia is where Warrington's twin town of Helden is located).

There is a selection of photographs from the Jubilee Parade in the colour photograph section at the centre of this book.

Mr. Maclean unveils the commemorative plaque outside reception

Jubilee Parade Colour Party passing the dais

2000 – 2006

Garry Insch, a security officer at Bruche recalled an incident that happened when he was on duty at the centre over a weekend, probably around 2002, although we haven't managed to pin it down to a specific date.

Garry was in the security lodge during the early evening, when he received a call asking for permission to land an RAF Sea King helicopter on the parade ground. The helicopter would be carrying a very sick baby, coming from a hospital in Newcastle upon Tyne, who was to receive some sort of a transplant at Warrington General Hospital.

The request was to land the helicopter, and an ambulance would then take the child to Warrington General Hospital for the transplant. Following the transplant, the child would be returned to the helicopter and flown back to Newcastle.

Garry managed (after some frantic phone calls!) to get permission from the Head of Centre for the helicopter to land and remain on the square for the required time.

The helicopter duly arrived, and the child was transferred to Warrington General Hospital. All went smoothly, although Garry wondered what the local residents must have thought when the helicopter began to warm up its engines at 4am the following morning, before it finally left at 5am – an unusual way to be woken up to say the least!

The Secret Policeman

The Secret Policeman was a BBC documentary, first shown on 23rd October 2003, with much footage shot at Bruche.

Mark Daly, the investigative reporter had joined the Greater Manchester Police as a recruit, to investigate racism in the police service.

An extract from his article on the BBC News Magazine website is reproduced below:

'It was at the Police National Training Centre in Warrington, where trainees from 10 forces in the North West and Wales spend 15 weeks that much of my material was garnered.

The extremity of some of the racism I encountered from these recruits beggared belief.

The majority of the officers I met will undoubtedly turn out to be good, non-prejudiced ones intent on doing the job properly. But the next generation of officers from one of Britain's top police colleges contains a significant minority of people who are holding the progress of the police service back.

Racist abuse like "Paki" and "Nigger" were commonplace for these PCs. The idea that white and Asian members of the public should be treated differently because of their colour was not only acceptable for some, but preferable. I had become a friend to these men. They trusted me with their views. And they believed I was one of them.

I operated under strict guidelines. I was not allowed to make racist comments or incite anyone to do or say anything which they wouldn't have otherwise said or done. But I had to laugh at their jokes and behave like a dumb apprentice. I said I was eager to hear other people's views in order to form my own. And they didn't hold back.

There is no doubt that this investigation will come under massive scrutiny from the police and the media - and rightly so.

The police say they are open and accountable to public scrutiny. If this is the case then they should welcome this investigation. And if the police have nothing to hide, then they would have nothing to fear. The decent officers out there, I hope, will support what I have done.

But there is no doubt that this programme will make some very uncomfortable viewing for the police service and the racists still in it'.

The Secret Policeman uncovered some extremely serious incidents of racist behaviour among some of the recruits who were at the centre with Mark Daly. Such behaviour, and extreme racist views have no place in today's police service, and do not fall within the definition of a police constable, which is at the front of this book.

However, I think it is important to consider these incidents in the overall context of Bruche as a police training centre.

I estimate that, since the centre opened in 1946, over 100,000 police officers, including recruits, instructors, and overseas students have passed through its doors and gone on to uphold the laws of this country, and others, in a fair and professional manner.

I believe that the extreme views and behaviour shown by the officers in the Secret Policeman exist in a very small minority of police officers, and that, to quote Mark Daly,

"The majority of the officers I met will undoubtedly turn out to be good, non-prejudiced ones intent on doing the job properly".

A friend and former colleague of mine at Bruche, Leo Simmons, saw the Secret Policeman documentary when it was screened by CBC TV in Canada in 2005, and wrote to the CBC to express his thoughts.

'Until April 30th 2002, I was a Police Officer in the Cheshire Constabulary. I left the service on that date, after eighteen years service, to leave the shores of the UK and begin a new life with my wife and children in Canada.

My final two and a half years service was in the role of a trainer/tutor at Bruche Police Training centre. My final thirty months in the UK police force, working at Bruche training centre, were perhaps the most fulfilling and enjoyable months of my career.

Training recruits is not glamorous, nor is it considered a particularly desirable career move, but it is in my opinion one of the most crucial roles a constable can undertake. My personal motivation for entering the training arena was a desire to make a difference, to try and ensure that the people I taught would be inspired to become the best police officers they could be, and the kind of officer the law-abiding public wish for.

I did that to the best of my ability, and I met many fine individuals who will, I am sure, go on to become excellent public servants, do great things, and make a positive difference to many.

Leo, class trainer with his last class of recruits on his final parade at Bruche in 2002, prior to leaving for Canada.

Final Parade

On 26th May 2006, the final parade was held at Bruche. The intake passing out on that date was Intake H 06, which had a complement of 92 officers. They were drawn from the forces of Staffordshire, Leicestershire, Derbyshire, West Mercia and West Midlands.

The weather during the whole of the parade was very wet, it rained continuously from beginning to end, and everyone involved got thoroughly soaked.

The Reviewing Officer for the parade was Mr. Norman Bettison, QPM, Chief Executive of Centrex, and a former Chief Constable of Merseyside Police, who has since been honoured with a knighthood in the 2006 Queen's Birthday Honours List.

Also present were police pensioner guests who did their initial training at Bruche in 1946. They were:

Albert Gaskin, formerly Manchester City Police, a student on Intake 1
Cyril Mills, formerly Liverpool City Police, also a student on Intake 1
Jenny Kewley, formally Blackpool Borough Police, a student on Intake 10

Principal guests at the parade were:

Deputy Chief Constable Christine Twigg, Cumbria Constabulary and Centrex Board Member
Commander Stuart Osborne, Deputy Director, Leadership Academy, Centrex
Superintendent Paul Finnegan, Head of Quality, Foundation Training, Centrex.

The Head of Centre, Chief Inspector Phil Jones delivered the last welcome speech to be made by a Bruche Head of Centre, during which he first apologised for the weather.

He went on to welcome over 500 former staff and students who had passed through the centre since the first course in 1946, including Bert Gaskin and Jenny Kewley, who both did their initial training at Bruche in 1946, and who were guests at the parade.

He also paid tribute to his staff at Bruche for their hard work and dedication to the business of the Centre.

Phil Jones introduces Norman Bettison (second from left) to the parade

Having inspected the students, who by this time were absolutely wet through, Mr. Bettison delivered the final speech by a Reviewing Officer of a parade at Bruche.

Recruits on the Final Parade listen to Norman Bettison's speech

He began by telling everyone not to feel sorry for the recruits who were standing out in the pouring rain, as they would have to get used to it over the next few years!

He said that, although Chief Inspector Jones had whispered in his ear about a 'smart speech' being appropriate in the dreadful conditions, he felt that as this was the final parade, he needed to do it justice, not just for Class H, but for all who had gone before them.

He went on:

"I wanted to make this world, the bit of the world that I policed, a slightly safer, happier, better place for the people that lived and worked and brought their children up there – and that's what connects me with every single one of you standing out there in the rain.

You have a commitment and a desire to reassure those who live in fear, to bring peace where there's disharmony and aggression, to bring justice on behalf of those who are wronged.

That's not some empty, idealistic concept, because the public that we serve are the people like your parents, loved ones, family and friends that are sheltering under the umbrellas and watching on proudly and damply from the sidelines.

It's that connection to public service that links us all here today. It links me with Bert Gaskin and Jenny Kewley, two of our great VIPs today. It's 60 years since each of them stood where you're standing now, but things aren't very different, they got wet then.

It's people that make the police service of England and Wales. Doing policing is about human interaction, and when you get out there on the streets, you won't prevent every crime, you won't catch every criminal, but 100% of the time every day, and at every incident, in every interaction you'll be courteous to the people who ask you to help and serve.

You'll show compassion, even if it's the 10th incident you're dealing with that day, it's the most traumatic thing that's happened to that person who looks to you for help, and you'll give it your integrity for the next 30 years, because Bert and Jenny would expect nothing less.

Each of these new recruits has been taught and supported by the staff at Bruche, who are second to none. If they've done their job right, they'll have passed over the baton of professional knowledge, but also the values and standards that will sustain you for the next 30 years.

Today's trainers (and they're dotted around, some of them in the rain, some of the more experienced under umbrellas), today's trainers stand as proxy for the long and proud traditions here at Bruche Police Training Centre, as do the administrative staff, as do the catering and housekeeping staff, and those people who've kept you fed and supported you and cared for you over the past 12 weeks, the porters and gardeners, the gardeners who don't have a job next week, who were out there for the last few days making this place look a picture.

They've all given their part to the 60 years of service that Bruche is proud of, and they're people just like you.

I want to thank, on your behalf, Phil Jones and his fantastic team, not just for what they've done in the last 12 weeks but for what they represent – the Bruche family - the Bruche family with its long and proud traditions.

Bruche Police Training Centre will close its gates forever as you leave here today. And for this brief and wet moment let us just take the opportunity to acknowledge what it's brought together on this parade square.

What it's brought together is the past, the present and the future, and most importantly the future of British policing.

Ladies and gentlemen, my newest colleagues – Class H of 2006 – it's you who have the furthest to go. As you turn to march off, this parade square will echo with the footfalls of those who have passed before you.

The echoes will fade, and what will be left are you, and you alone, to carry the reputation of Bruche Training Centre and the British police service.

We want you, your trainers and those who've supported you, your parents, your loved ones, your family, we want you to do just one thing for us. What we want is, everyday that you put on that uniform, to do something that makes us proud.

Class H of 2006 – God speed and I wish you every success.'

Commandants at Bruche

Percy Hawkins	Glossop	1946 – 1954
F. A. Seward	Metropolitan Police	1954 – 1959
J. H. Thompson	Southport Borough	1959 – 1962
G. T. Saunders	Rochdale Borough	1962 – 1964
W. J Ross	St. Helens Borough	1964 – 1966
K. E. Smith	Oldham Borough	1966 – 1970
R. W. Stone	Devon & Cornwall	1970 – 1972
A. M. Hayward	Gwent	1972 – 1974
W. Hadfield	GMP	1974 – 1977
J. Colledge	Merseyside	1977 – 1979
R. Stainton	Cumbria	1980 – 1983
H. Mather	Lancs	1983 – 1986
T. McCabe	GMP	1986 – 1989
J. A. Hewer	Merseyside	1989 – 1994
P. W. Kinson	GMP	1994 – 1999
P. A. Taylor	Durham	1999 – 2004
P. K. Jones	N. Wales	2004 – 2006

The Spirit of Bruche

In conclusion, I felt I had to write the final few words of my book about the spirit of Bruche, to try to sum up what its long and proud traditions mean for all those whose lives have been touched by the place and its people.

How do I encapsulate the great history and traditions of Bruche, the spirit of the place, the tears and laughter that have echoed around its walls for over 60 years? The family atmosphere, the camaraderie, and the contribution that Bruche has made to so many, many lives – not just the people who have trained or worked there, but to all whose lives have been touched by staff and students from Bruche?

The spirit of Bruche is shown by the US aircraft technicians who bravely volunteered to travel to an unknown destination to help keep the aircraft flying during the Second World War.

It is shown by the many friendships made among police recruits, instructors, trainers and support staff who passed through Bruche, and which still flourish today.

It exists in the bravery of many of the police officers who left Bruche and went on to risk their own lives in order to help others, and to demonstrate the highest standards of policing in their efforts to preserve law and order.

It is shown by the day to day dealings with people, by police officers who passed through Bruche, and who now perform their duties as professional police officers, trained to a high standard, while maintaining compassion and empathy for those they come into contact with.

The spirit of Bruche will continue, even if the site is demolished, because it is not just the place, it is the people who made it what it was, and it is people whose memories and friendships will carry its great history and traditions forward during the years to come.

I hope you enjoy my book.

I will be assisting the Greater Manchester Police Museum to compile an archive of Bruche, to preserve its history and to enable research in the future.

If you would like to contribute any photographs or information to this archive, please contact the museum, details below:

Greater Manchester Police Museum
Newton Street
Manchester
M1 1ES

Tel: 0161 856 3287
Email: policemuseum@gmp.police.uk